On F
Throu
Euro
A TRAIL GUIDE TO
SPAIN & PORTUGAL

ALSO INCLUDES: *Andorra, The Azores, The Canary Islands, Madeira and Mallorca*

Here's What Europe's Walking Organizations Say About this Book

"The most complete reference for the hiker in Germany." —LUDWIG LENZ, 3rd Direktor, Deutscher Alpenverein (German Alpine Club), Munich.

"Extraordinarily comprehensive." —JOHN NEWNHAM, assistant secretary, The Ramblers' Association, London.

"Excellent. Many more or less experienced alpinists could learn quite a lot on how to prepare a tour and on what to do in cases of emergency."— LUCETTE DUVOISIN, general secretary, Schweizerische Arbeitsgemeinschaft für Wanderwege (Swiss Footpath Protection Association), Basel.

"A very comprehensive and most valuable book." —DR. SONJA JORDAN, Österreichische Fremdenverkehrswerbung (Austrian National Tourist Office), Vienna.

"I was very impressed. This book will be of great value to all hikers who want to go to other countries." —FINN HAGEN, Den Norske Turistforening (Norwegian Mountain Touring Association), Oslo.

"You've done a helluva good job assembling and organizing a truly awesome amount of data. You seem to have thought of every contingency—and then some—so the prospective walker will be able to plan his vacation well in advance of departure. . . . This guide should become something of a classic in its field—a backpacker's Baedeker." —STEPHEN R. WHITNEY, former managing editor, Sierra Club Books, and author of *A Sierra Club Naturalist's Guide: The Sierra Nevada*.

"Your work is very complete and accurate (something we find seldom, even in our own country)." —FREDDY TUERLINCKX, general secretary, Grote Routepaden (Long-Distance Footpath Association), Antwerp.

"I am really impressed with the enormous work that you have been able to do in a short time—and by the amount of knowledge and experience that you show!" —INGEMUND HÄGG, Svenska turistföreningen (Swedish Touring Club), Stockholm.

"A Bible of European hiking opportunities." —EDWARD B. GARVEY, member of the Appalachian Trail Council Board of Managers and author of *Appalachian Hiker: Adventure of a Lifetime.*

On Foot Through Europe

A TRAIL GUIDE TO SPAIN & PORTUGAL

ALSO INCLUDES: *Andorra, The Azores, The Canary Islands, Madeira and Mallorca*

by Craig Evans

Walking, Backpacking, Ski Touring, Climbing—Everything You Can Do On Foot

QUILL
New York 1982

Library of Congress Catalog Card Number: 82-603

ISBN: 0-688-01195-0 (pbk)

Printed in the United States of America

First Quill Edition

1 2 3 4 5 6 7 8 9 10

Behind the Scenes

M ANY PEOPLE HAVE contributed to this book—people in tourist offices, weather bureaus, forestry services, sport shops, guidebook and map outlets and tour organizations. In addition, the members of Spain's mountaineering federations have been especially helpful. Without the assistance of these people—and the time and effort they devoted to answering questions, researching information and reviewing the final manuscript—this book would not have been possible.

To all who helped prepare the manuscript—typists, translators, proofreaders, friends—I also owe my sincere gratitude.

And to those who helped the most, a special thanks:

For reviewing the entire manuscript, helping offset my American bias and providing otherwise hard-to-get information:

Arthur Howcroft, president of the European Ramblers' Assocation's Walking Committee and a tour leader for England's Country-Wide Holidays Association.

Ingemund Hägg, secretary of the European Ramblers' Association's Walking Committee, consultant to the Svenska turistföreningen (Swedish Touring Club) and author of *Walking in Europe,* a 40-page booklet on where to get information to go walking in 25 countries, published in English by the Swedish Touring Club, 1978 (a handy booklet, incidentally, that is well worth owning).

For providing information on walking in their areas and for reviewing for accuracy the chapters on their countries:

ANDORRA

Roser Jordana de Madero, Sindicat d'Iniciativa de les Valla d'Andorra, Andorra la Vella.
Joan Prat, Club Pirinenc Andorra, Les Escaldes.

THE AZORES

Maria do Carmo Franco Fernandes, Delegação de Turismo de São Miguel, Ponta Delgada.

CANARY ISLANDS

Mario Rial Gonzáles, Ministerio de Información y Turismo, Santa Cruz de Tenerife.

MADEIRA

Mário Saraiva, Direcção Geral do Turismo, Lisbon.

MALLORCA

Pere Llofriu Mora, Federación Española de Montañismo, Delegacíon en Baleares, Palma de Mallorca.

PORTUGAL

Nuno Almeida, director, Portuguese National Tourist Office, New York.
Maria Helena Pereira Dias, Direcção Geral do Ondenamento Gestão Florestal, Lisbon.
Mário Saraiva, Direção Geral do Turismo, Lisbon.

SPAIN

Juan Cullel-Altimiras, president, Comité Nacional de Senderos de Gran Recorrido, Federación Español de Montañismo, Barcelona.
Aurelio Castillo and *Francisco A. Olmedo,* Federación Andaluza de Montañismo, Granada.
Joaquín Cano Díz, president, Federación Leonesa de Montañismo, León.
Juan R. Lozano, Comité de Senderos de Gran Recorrido, Federación Castellana de Montañismo, Madrid.
Edmund Mireles, American Embassy, Madrid.
Ramon Ramon Maisonave, Comité Senderos Gran Recorrido, Federación Aragonesa de Montañismo, Zaragoza.
Manuel Alvarez Martínez, Federación Asturiana de Montañismo, Oviedo.
Charles Ocheltree, Spanish National Tourist Office, New York.
Domingo Pliego, Federación Castellana de Montañismo, Madrid.
Joan Quera, Llibreria Quera, Barcelona.
Enric Aguadé Sans, president, Comissió de Promoció d'Excursions, Comité Catalá de Senders de Gran Recorregut, Federació d'Entitas Excursionistes de Catalunya, Reus.

There was also the enormous dedication of the people who made the trail guide series come to physical reality. The basic team was: Ed Meehan who drew the maps, Brian Sheridan who did the illustrations, Vincent Torre who designed the cover and Elisabeth Kofler Shuman, my research and editorial assistant.

There was also Stephen R. Whitney, my editor, whose involvement in this book escalated far beyond that of simply an editor, and whose commitment to its completion became much more than he—or his wife—ever bargained for. As deadlines approached and the size of each chapter swelled, he evolved from copy editor and devil's advocate to co-author, writing first short sections of unfinished chapters from my notes, then whole chapters. And I, in turn, became his rewriter and editor. Together, we were able to complete seven books, ensure their accuracy and oversee every detail of their production, a job I could never have accomplished alone and still have met the final deadline.

Finally, there was William Kemsley, Jr., president of Foot Trails Publications, Inc., whose own passion for detail sustained his unfaltering belief in this trail guide series through all of its growing pains, despite the advice of his accountants. Few publishers would have put up with so much when lesser books could have been produced more economically. Yet he rarely asked that compromises be made. He only asked that it be done. And done well.

Thank you, each of you. You've been great friends.

Craig Evans
Washington, D.C., 1981

How to Use this Book

THIS BOOK IS PACKED with information. It describes every aspect of walking, backpacking and climbing in Andorra, the Azores, the Canary Islands, Madeira, Mallorca, Portugal and Spain: all the places you can go, the maps and guidebooks you need, where you can get information on trail lodgings and camping, the weather conditions you can expect and the telephone numbers to call for weather forecasts. There's even a list of special train and bus fares that can save you money. And more: the clothing and equipment you will need, where equipment shops are located, walking tours you might like to take advantage of, even some tidbits of history and folklore.

There are also hundreds of addresses—places you can write for maps and guidebooks, obtain train and bus schedule information and get specific answers on walking and traveling in particular areas. And you get a lot more than an address. Everything is spelled out: the information and services available, the languages in which inquires can be made and, if useful publications are available, what their titles are and what information they contain.

The result is a complete sourcebook to all the information available on walking, backpacking, ski touring and climbing in Iberia.

This book has been designed to make finding the specific information you need as easy as possible. The table of contents lists the major divisions in each chapter, plus some minor divisions, so you can turn right to the page where, say, the services provided by the walking organizations or the emergency telephone numbers for search and rescue are given. The name of each organization has been set off from the rest of the text by means of a darker type face and additional spacing so it can be found easily—again and again. And all the addresses and telephone numbers are listed in an alphabetical *Address Directory* at the back of each chapter so you have only one place to look when you need to use one. There is even a section entitled *A Quick Reference* at the end of the chapters on each country, which gives you the page numbers where the most important information is located on walking in that country.

The area codes for all telephone numbers have been listed in parenthesis. For example, the number listed for the Federación Española de Montañismo in Madrid is (91) 445 13 82. (91) is the area code.

- To reach this number from within the same area—say, Madrid itself—omit the area code and dial only the telephone number: 445 13 82.
- To reach this number from a different area within the same country—say, Barcelona—dial the entire number as shown (91) 445 13 82.
- To reach this number from a different country—say, Switzerland—first refer to the front pages to find the appropriate country code for Spain. From Switzerland this number is 00 34 Next, dial the area code *minus* the initial numeral: (1). Then dial the telephone number: 445 13 82. Hence: 00 34 (1) 445 13 82.

Another help: this book was bound so you can remove pages—and thus save lugging the entire book along—when you just want one chapter on the trail for easy reference. To remove pages: 1) open the book to the first page you wish to remove; 2) bend the book open as far as it will go; 3) turn to the end of the section you wish to remove; 4) again, bend the book open as far as it will go; 5) with one hand, hold down the pages on either side of the section you wish to remove; 6) with the thumb and index finger of the other hand, grasp the top part of the section at the point where it attaches to the spine, and 7) slowly pull the section away from the spine. The pages should come out in a complete section, with all the pages attached to one another.

When you wish to return a chapter you have removed to the book, simply slip it back into the space where it belongs. Then put a rubber band around the book so the loose sections don't fall out.

Finally, one last note: every attempt has been made to ensure the information in this book is both complete and accurate. Nonetheless, those who worked on the book—myself, the reviewers in each country, copy editors and typesetters—are not perfect. An occasional mistake might have slipped past. Two numerals is a telephone number might have been transposed and never caught. A name may have been mispelled or a valuable guidebook overlooked. If so, it was not intentional.

There are the inevitable changes to consider, too. All addresses, telephone numbers and prices were verified prior to publication. But people and organizations move, telephone numbers change and prices go up. Hence, I cannot accept responsibility or liability for any inaccuracies or ommissions.

Prices, of course, change constantly. *Those quoted are meant only as guides.* For each year after 1981, expect a yearly increase of *at least 15 percent.* Maybe more.

This book describes the opportunities in the different regions of Spain and Portugal. Six other books cover the rest of Europe:

- *On Foot Through Europe: A Trail Guide to Austria, Switzerland & Liechtenstein*
- *On Foot Through Europe: A Trail Guide to the British Isles*

- *On Foot Through Europe: A Trail Guide to Scandinavia*
- *On Foot Through Europe: A Trail Guide to West Germany*
- *On Foot Through Europe: A Trail Guide to France & the Benelux Nations*

Use this or any of the area guides in conjunction with *On Foot Through Europe: A Trail Guide to Europe's Long-Distance Footpaths,* which gives you an overview of walking in Europe and tips on how to plan your hikes. All the background information available—and the places where you can get it—is here. It includes how to get information by mail, how to get to and stay along the trails, how to follow the paths safely, what to do in an emergency, and what equipment to bring, and many other facts to get you started hiking through Europe.

I welcome your comments. If you find an address or telephone number has changed, or you think some additional information should have been included in the book and was not, please let me know. Write to me at: Foot Trails Publications, Inc., Bedford Road, Greenwich, Connecticut 06830 U.S.A.

Contents

Where & How to Go
Hiking
in Spain
and Portugal

Difficulty:
What the Footpath Gradings Mean

The footpaths described in this book have been graded according to their difficulty. These gradings are based upon the *Schwierigkeitsgrade*—or difficulty gradings—developed for walkers in Austria. They are:

Easy (Schwierigkeitsgrad A & B). A path across either level or gently undulating terrain. Differences in altitude are small—less than 250 meters. The path requires minimal effort. It can be walked in any weather. Suitable for families with young children.

Easy to Moderately Difficult (Schwierigkeitsgrad C). A path across hilly terrain or mountains of medium height (up to 1,800 meters in altitude). The path presents few complications: climbs and descents are rarely steep, altitude differences are less than 600 meters and route finding is generally not difficult. Except in extremely bad weather, the path can be walked without great effort.

Moderately Difficult (Schwierigkeitsgrad D). A path with regular climbs and descents. Sections of the path may cross steep, rocky or marshy terrain. Some sections may also be above treeline or partially obstructed with undergrowth. The path generally can be walked without difficulty in good weather—providing you are physically fit, have the proper equipment and know how to use a map and compass. In bad weather use caution. Check with local authorities before you set out to be sure you are aware of any peculiarities in the local weather and path conditions.

Difficult (Schwierigkeitsgrad E). A strenuous route across rough terrain. Climbs and descents are steep and difficult. Precipices, swiftly flowing streams, thick undergrowth or snowfields may be encountered. In some places use of a map and compass may be essential to follow the route. On particularly exposed or dangerous sections safety devices—such as fixed cables and ladders—may be installed along the path. No climbing skills nor climbing equipment are required. Sections of some routes, however, will require that you are sure footed and are not subject to acrophobia. Novices and families with young children should not attempt such a route. In bad weather, *all* walkers should avoid it.

For Experienced Mountain Walkers Only (Schwierigkeitsgrad F). An extremely difficult route—across glaciers, on routes with exposed or dangerous sections (and no fixed cables or other safety devices), or cross-country through rough terrain where accurate route-finding with a map and compass is essential. Climbs and descents are steep and treacherous and may require rock climbing (up to Class II). Stream crossings are tricky and may require use of a rope. Severe, quick-changing weather conditions also may be encountered. To follow this route mountaineering experience is imperative, as is specialized equipment—crampons, ice axe or rope—and knowledge of its use.

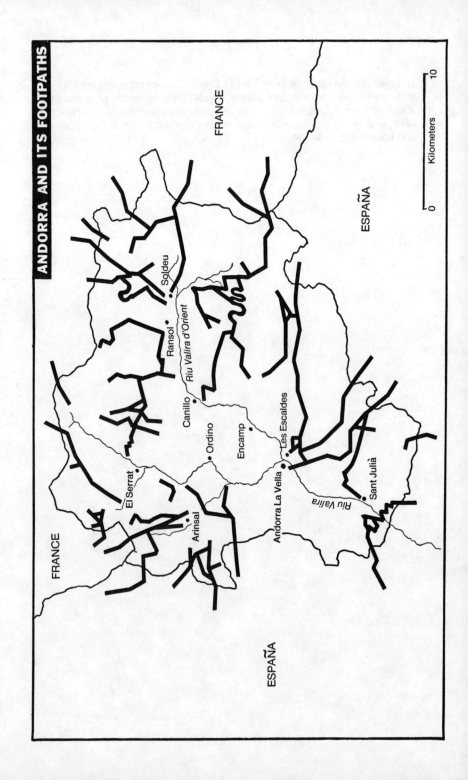

ANDORRA AND ITS FOOTPATHS

FRANCE

FRANCE

ESPAÑA

ESPAÑA

Soldeu

Ransol

Riu Valira d'Orient

Canillo

Ordino

Encamp

El Serrat

Arinsal

Andorra La Vella

Les Escaldes

Riu Valira

Sant Julià

0   Kilometers   10

Andorra

ANDORRA IS A TINY, yet enchanting land. Its 464 square kilometers (188 square miles) encompass seven valleys, four rivers, a thermal spring, more than 80 lakes and 65 peaks in excess of 2,500 meters (8,202 feet) high.

Napoleon is said to have found the country so appealing he wanted it preserved as a museum piece. And indeed, its old stone villages, its Romanesque bell towers and the lichen-encrusted stone walls that lace its hillsides, enclosing solitary farmhouses, are now being preserved.

But Andorra has also become commercialized. Only 4 percent of its land area is suitable for agriculture, and its location—in the eastern Pyrenees between Spain and France—is not conducive to the establishment of most forms of industry. So, Andorra has become instead a tourist center. Also, it imposes only token taxes and duties, which allow merchants to offer low prices. As a result, stores bulge with radios and cameras from Japan, cigars from Brazil, peasant skirts from Afghanistan and liquors from around the world—all at prices attractive enough to make a trip to the mini mountain-top country worthwhile.

The commercialization, however, is limited primarily to the main street of the capital, Andorra la Vella. The rest of the country is filled with mountains, deep forests of pine and birch, tobacco fields and meadows sprinkled with wildflowers.

People are friendly, if somewhat reserved. Most of the 30,000 inhabitants are descended from an ancient people initially composed of shepherds, ironmongers and mountain porters, and they still preserve their centuries-old customs. According to legend, Andorra was founded in the year 784 by Charlemagne. It is now a principality. The country employs 42 policemen, has no army and has never had a war. It has no customs check points. Catalan is the official language, but Spanish and French are also spoken. Everything is communally owned except for buildings and farmland. And political campaigns for membership on the ruling General Council are unknown; a candidate who files for office is simply assessed by the citizenry in casual café conversations.

Distances are short. Andorra is less than 30 kilometers in both width and length. In a day and a half you can walk across the country, although to do so you must cross up to three mountain ranges, climb a total of more than 3,200 meters (10,500 feet) and descend another 3,100 meters (10,170

5

feet). The lowest point—along the Valira River at Andorra's southern border with Spain—is more than 800 meters (2,625 feet) above sea level. Three peaks rise above 2,900 meters, the highest of which is 2,946-meter (9,665-foot) Coma Pedrosa near the country's western border with France. There are also sheer cliffs and rock walls to challenge climbers.

For walkers, there are more than 300 kilometers of trails crisscrossing the country. Villages where food and lodging can be found are always within reach. And there is an abundance of wildlife—chamois, wild boar, mountain goat, deer, rabbit, partridge and an occasional eagle.

Climate

Despite Andorra's small size, temperatures and rainfall can vary greatly from one locale to another within the country. The town of Ransol, for instance, receives an average of 1,071 mm (42 inches) of precipitation per year, while the town of Escaldes, 11 kilometers by road to the south and 600 meters lower in elevation, receives an annual average of only 890 mm (35 inches) of precipitation—17 percent less.

Average daytime temperatures in the country range from a high in August of 26°C. (79°F.), to a low in January of 8°C. (46.4°F.). Average nighttime temperatures for August are 15°C. (59°F.) and for January, *minus* 17°C. (1.4°F.). But these are averages.

Typically, Pyrenean summer days are hot and vulnerable to late afternoon thunderstorms, while temperatures can plummet below freezing at night. For this reason, early starts each day are advisable, as is sensible attire—a sunhat for the morning, raingear for the afternoon and warm clothing at night.

In late spring and early autumn heavy rains can last for several days and may dump snow in the mountains. Winter nights are often bitterly cold, although the days are usually crisp and clear—ideal for walking from January to April

Still, at any time, the weather can change quickly.

Even though you never will be far from shelter while walking in Andorra, it is essential to always carry warm clothing, a windbreaker and raingear.

It is also advisable to obtain a weather forecast before you set out. You can do this by calling the *Sindicat d'Iniciativa*—the tourist office. Its telephone number is: 20214. Or you can call:

Pronóstico del tiempo: Tel. 21166. Forecasts are given in Catalan and French. Or:

Pronóstico del tiempo: Tel. 21055. Forecasts are given in Catalan and Spanish.

Where to Get Walking Information

Enquiries about walking in Andorra are handled by the tourist office. Unfortunately, the office is not good about providing many details about walking by letter. Once you are in the country, however, its staff can answer most questions you have:

Sindicat d'Iniciativa de les Valls d'Andorra (for its address and telephone number, see the *Address Directory* at the back of this chapter). The office staff speaks English, Spanish, French, Catalan, Italian and Portuguese.

In addition, Andorra has a small mountaineering club. It does not answer enquiries about walking in Andorra. But you can obtain information on the club and its activities by writing:

Club Pirinenc Andorrà (see *Address Directory*). Staff speaks Catalan, Spanish and French.

Maps & Guidebooks

One of the few sources of information on walking in Andorra is a small guidebook and map published in Catalan:

- *Andorra—i Sectors Fronterers d'Alt Urgell i Cerdanya*, Editorial Alpina, Granollers, Spain. Includes a 32-page description of Andorra's history, geography, climate, culture and economy as well as suggestions for 14 day-long hikes and several short excursions. Brief information on the mountain shelters in Andorra, and those across the border in Spain, is also included. A separate, five-color topographical map accompanies the booklet. The map is drawn in a scale of 1:40,000 and shows the locations of all the trails and mountain shelters in Andorra. However, it also contains several inaccuracies.

The booklet is simply written and short enough so that it is possible to understand most of the information on the hikes and shelters without knowing Catalan. Summaries of the information also appear in Spanish and French.

One other excellent guidebook covers Andorra:

- *Cerdanya* (in Spanish) by Augustí Jolis and M.ª Antònia Simó de Jolis, Colección de Guías del Centre Excursionista de Catalunya, Club

Alpí Catalá, Editorial Montblanc, Barcelona, Spain. Provides exhaustive coverage of Andorra and the surrounding mountain regions to the east. Includes dozens of route descriptions, as well as information on geography, geology, climate, flora, fauna and mountain refuges. Also describes cross-country ski routes and winter ascents. Each walk description gives the walking time required for the entire route, as well as the times it takes to get from one point to the next along the way. Climbing routes are rated according to difficulty and are shown on excellent line drawings of the various massifs. Sketch maps showing walking routes are also included. (Recommended)

Neither guidebook can be purchased in Andorra, but only by mail from:

Llibreria Quera (see *Address Directory*). You may write in English, French or Spanish. Responses, however, will be in Spanish.

Maps in a scale of 1:50,000 are published by:

Instituto Geográfico y Catastral (see *Address Directory*).

Because these maps are laid out in quadrants, it requires four of the maps to cover Andorra—sheets 182 *Tirvia*, 183 *Andorra*, 215 *Seo de Urgel* and 216 *Bellver*. These maps are also available by mail from the *Llibreria Quera*.

A much better alternative is to buy the five-color topographical maps published by *M.I. Consell General d'Andorra:*

- *Valls d'Andorra*, 1:50,000. One sheet covering all of Andorra. An excellent map for hiking. Includes an index to the 1:10,000 sheets covering Andorra.
- *Mapes Oficials d'Andorra*, 1:10,000. A series of 19 sheets covering Andorra. Well suited for climbing.

All the M.I. Consell General maps have been revised in the last five years. They can be purchased from all the bookshops in Andorra, as well as by mail from the tourist office.

Trailside Lodgings

For the most part, the mountain shelters in Andorra consist of cabañas—small stone shelters used by shepherds. These sleep three people and are really only suitable for an emergency "bivvy." They have no wardens, no food and no cooking facilities. They also don't have blankets, so if you are caught by bad weather on the trail and have to hole up in one, you'll appreciate a lot of extra warm clothing in your pack.

In addition to the cabañas, Andorra has more than 200 hotels and pensions. Two of these are located on trails near Grau Roig and Port d'Envalira, two of the country's ski areas.

Adjacent to Andorra, there are several *refugios* that have been built by a variety of Spanish clubs in the major climbing areas. These huts are free, usually well kept and can sleep about 20 people. Although they have neither wardens nor food, some do have a stock of blankets. But you cannot always depend upon this. Also, not all of the huts are open all year. In France, there are several unstaffed refuges, plus an occasional refuge based on alpine standards—with a warden and hot meals.

The locations of the cabañas and several of the refugios surrounding Andorra are indicated on the 1:40,000 map that accompanies the Editorial Alpina booklet, *Andorra*. But before you start up the trail, it is advisable to check up on the refugios and cabañas you wish to use—find out if they are open, if the map references are reliable and if it is a Spanish holiday (in which case abandon all hope of a quiet night's sleep).

Information on Andorra's cabañas—as well as on its hotels and pensions—can be obtained from the tourist office.

Camping

There are 26 commercial campgrounds in Andorra, most of which have showers, grocery stores and restaurants. Five even have swimming pools. A list is available from the tourist office.

Camping along the trails outside of the campgrounds is not allowed. You can, however, pitch a tent in a pasture—providing you obtain prior permission from the farmer who owns it.

Water

Animals are plentiful at high altitudes. More than 1,500 cows and nearly 35,000 sheep graze in the high meadows during the summer. As a result, you should not drink indiscriminately from rivers and streams at low altitudes. Springs are safe thirst quenchers. So is tap water and water from drinking trough spouts, unless posted with a sign that says: *aigua non potable*. At high altitudes, use discretion. Many high altitude lakes and streams are crystal pure. Those that drain the high pastures, however, are not.

Walking Tours

Several European organizations offer walking tours in Andorra. Among them:

Ramblers' Holidays Ltd. (see *Address Directory*).

Inside Andorra, most tour excursions are by bus or jeep. A few are combined with several hours of walking to reach high-level lakes, but none are devoted solely to walking.

Information on the excursions is available from the tourist office as well as from the local travel agencies that run the tours:

See *Address Directory*:

Andotour in Les Escaldes.

Excursions Coll in Andorra la Vella.

Excursions Font in Les Escaldes.

Excursions Lito in Andorra la Vella.

Pantours in Andorra la Vella.

Viatges Evisa-Cadotur in Les Escaldes.

Viatges Popular in Andorra la Vella.

Viatges Relax in Andorra la Vella.

Guides & Mountaineering Courses

Mountain guides for a climb of one of Andorra's peaks are available on request through the tourist office. Before attempting a climb you should have prior experience. There are no climbing schools in Andorra to teach you the necessary techniques.

Ski Touring & Ski Mountaineering

The mountains of Andorra are snow-covered for six and a half months of the year—from November until May. Most of the skiing is limited to the downhill ski runs at Andorra's five ski areas. But cross-country skiing is becoming popular, and there are marked tracks at Solden and Grau-Roig. Elsewhere, you should first check with the tourist office—or the ski club—to find out where you can and cannot go ski touring. By following snow-covered jeep roads, it is possible to make a ski trek across Andorra. But ski mountaineers are pretty much on their own, although advice on possible routes and areas where avalanche dangers are high can be obtained from the ski club:

Esqui Club d'Andorra (see *Address Directory*). You can write to the office in Spanish, French or Catalan.

Two guidebooks to ski mountaineering routes in Andorra are also available:

- *Fixtes Esquí: Pic de la Serrera* and *Fixtes Esquí: Pic de la Coma Pedrosa* (in Catalan, Spanish and French) both by Enric Font, Xavier Gregori and Joseph M. Sala of the Centre Excursionista de Catalunya in Barcelona, Editorial Alpina, Granollers, Spain. Two in a series of guides describing ski touring routes, climbs and traverses in the Pyrenees. Each route is fully described and includes a sketch map, information on its difficulty, skiing time and a list of the required topographical maps. The geography of the region is also briefly described. Available from Llibreria Quera, Barcelona.

Emergency Telephone Numbers

In case of an accident in the mountains, you should call the police from the nearest telephone:

Police Emergency: Tel. 21222. The police generally understand Spanish, French, English and Catalan.

To find out about **avalanche hazards** in the winter: Tel. 20214.

Transportation in Andorra

Bus service between the main villages in Andorra is provided by a fleet of microbuses. There is no fixed time schedule.

How to Get There

Trains connect with daily bus service to Andorra from four towns in France and one town in Spain. There is also twice-daily coach service from Barcelona, Spain.

In France, buses to Andorra depart from:

Ax-les-Thermes. Daily service from May 1 to October 1. The afternoon departure is from the bus terminal at the main square.

L'Hospitalet. Year-round service. Daily departure from the train station immediately after the arrival of the morning train from Toulouse.

La Tour de Carol. Daily service from April 1 to November 30. Departures from the Gare Internationale.

Bourg-Madame. From the train station, walk toward the Pont Internationale (International Bridge), pass through French and Spanish customs and cross into Spain to catch the bus from Puigcerdà. There are five daily buses from Puigcerdà.

These towns can be reached by train from:

Paris (*Gare d'Austerlitz*). By express train to Toulouse. To avoid a change of train in Toulouse, board one of the through carriages that connect with the *Toulouse, Foix, Bourg-Madame, Perpignan* service.

Italy and the French Riviera. By train via Narbonne and Perpignan to Bourg-Madame or La Tour de Carol.

In Spain, buses for Andorra depart from:

Puigcerdà. Five buses daily. Year-round service. Board the bus for La Seu d'Urgell at the bus terminal. At La Seu d'Urgell change to the Andorra bus.

Puigcerdà can be reached by train from Barcelona.

All buses terminate in Andorra la Vella. Return bus service to these towns leave from Plaça Guillemo in Andorra la Vella. Timetables should be checked at your departure point. They change from season to season.
Coach service is available from:

Barcelona. Year-round service. Run by Co. Hispano-Andorrana. Daily departures from Ronad Universitat, 4.

Address Directory

A

- *Andotour,* Avinguda Carlemany 35, Les Escaldes. Tel. 21138.

C

- *Centre Excursionista de Catalunya,* Barcelona, Editorial Alpina, Granollers.
- *Club Pirinenc Andorrà,* Edific: Atlas 2 = 2·, Les Escaldes.
- *Colección de Guias del Centre Excursionista de Catalunva,* Club Alpí Catalá, Editorial Montblanc, Barcelona, Spain.

E

- *Editorial Alpina,* Apartado de Correos 3, Granollers, Spain.
- *Emergency:* Tel. 21222. To find out about avalanche hazards in the winter: Tel. 20214.
- *Esqui Club d-Andorra,* Urbanitzacio Babot, Andorra la Vella. Tel. 20010.
- *Excursions Coll,* Avinguda Meritxell 63, Andorra la Vella. Tel. 20091.
- *Excursions Font,* Avinguda Sant Juame, Les Escaldes. Tel. 21138.
- *Excursions Lito,* Aviguda Meritxell 63, Andorra la Vella. Tel. 20000.

I

- *Instituto Geografico y Catastral,* Calle General Ibane de Ibero 3, Madrid 3, Spain.

L

- *Llibreria Quera,* Petritxol 2, Barcelona 2, Spain.

P

- *Pantours,* Plaça Rebés 11, Andorra la Vella. Tel. 20434.

R

- *Ramblers' Holidays Ltd.* 13 Longcroft House, Eretherne Road, Welwyn Garden City, Hertfordshire AL8 6PQ, England.

S

- *Sindicat d'Inicjativa de les Valls d'Andorra,* Plaça Prícep Benlloch 1, Andorra la Vella. Tel. 21214.

V

- *Viatges Evisa-Cadotur,* Avinguda Carlemany 38, Les Escaldes. Tel. 21730 or 21316.
- *Viatges Popular,* Plaça Princep Benlloch 6, Andorra la Vella. Tel. 21359.
- *Viatges Relax,* Carrer Roc dels Escolls 12, Andorra la Vella. Tel. 20595 or 22044 or 22055.

W

- *Weather Forecast:* Pronóstico del tiempo: Tel. 21166. Forecasts are given in Catalan and French, or: Pronóstico del tiempo: Tel. 21055. Forecasts are given in Catalan and Spanish.

A Quick Reference

In a hurry? Turn to the pages listed below. They will give you the most important information on walking in Andorra.

Weather Forecasts, page 6.

Associations to Contact for Information:
On Walking, page 7.
On Skiing, page 10.

Maps & Guidebooks, page 7.

Equipment: See the comments under *Climate,* page 6.

Address Directory, page 13.

The Azores

THE AZORES OFFER numerous possibilities for short hikes, many of which can be combined with snorkeling and scuba diving, exploring volcanoes and subterranean caves, or simply basking on a sandy beach beneath towering vine-covered cliffs on a secluded inlet.

Located in the mid-Atlantic—1,225 kilometers (760 miles) from Lisbon and 3,400 kilometers (2,110 miles) from New York—the Azores comprise nine semitropical islands—Santa Maria, São Miguel, Terceira, Graciosa, São Jorge, Pico, Faial, Flores and Corvo. The coastlines of the islands feature coves, cliffs and crescent-shaped beaches of white, black and golden sand. Inland, the ruins of 16th century forts exist side by side with white villages and vineyards and fields of sugar beets, tea and chicory. Oxcarts move slowly along winding, flower-lined roads. And on the hilltops, the revolving white sails of windmills turn lava millstones that grind the corn.

Paths on the islands pass through semitropical forests of huge ferns and fig trees, across lava flows and along small belvederes perched high above the sea. They lead you past small lagoons and waterfalls, up mountains and to the brinks of craters. Some of the craters are filled with steaming fumaroles and geysers; others are carpeted with lush vegetation and dotted with lakes. Few paths are more than 15 kilometers in length, although several paths and mule tracks can sometimes be linked up for longer walks.

Little information on walking in the islands is available. There is no hiking organization in the Azores, and no guidebooks are published to the trails. Tourist brochures and guides tend to concentrate on excursions by car. Only occasionally do they hint that a tourist can get out of the car and walk.

One advantage of this is that the paths are relatively uncrowded. But as a walker, you are pretty much on your own. Once you are in the Azores, the three tourist bureaus on the islands can suggest walks and tell you how to get to the various trails. But even then, details may be sketchy. It is best to plan your own routes and then check these with the tourist offices before you set out.

A good, up-to-date series of 1:50,000 maps of the islands show most of the footpaths. Despite a lack of markings, most paths are clear-cut. Even so, forest paths that have fallen into disuse quickly become overgrown. In

THE AZORES

CORVO

FLORES

Atlantic Ocean

GRACIOSA
Praia

TERCEIRA
Angra do Heroísmo

SÃO JORGE
Calheta
V.a das Velas

FAIAL
Horta

PICO
Lajes

SÃO MIGUEL
Ponta Delgada

SANTA MARIA
V.a do Porto

KILOMETERS
0   100

Atlantic Ocean

CANADA

UNITED STATES

BRITAIN

FRANCE

SPAIN

PORTUGAL

AFRICA

THE AZORES

areas where there is little undergrowth it is also possible to walk cross-country. But here, if you plan to cross private property, you will have to get the landowner's prior permission.

The tourist offices can also help you take advantage of all the other activities on the islands—the numerous religious festivals, as well as deep sea fishing, sailing and scuba diving. There are also whalers on the islands who still hunt the endangered mammals from small boats with hand-thrown harpoons. And the island of Terceira features the *tourada à corda* —a bullfight in which the bull, instead of being killed, is returned to pasture after its horn-tossing run through village streets. During its run, the bull is partially controlled by a long rope—hence the name of the sport. Even so, the best place to observe the bull's run is from the safety of a balcony.

Flora & Fauna

The fertile soil and mild climate of the Azores support abundant vegetation. The island flora includes several native species that are elsewhere extinct as well as exotic plants and trees from all over the world.

In fact, the Azores have become a vast acclimatization garden since their discovery by the Portuguese in 1427. Because of their geographical location, the islands were for a long time an important port of call for ships bound for the New World as well as for those returning from India. As a result, many diverse plants and animals were imported to the islands.

Here are to be seen Mediterranean pines, lime and plane trees from northern Europe, cedars of Lebanon, tulip trees, camphor trees from the Far East, tropical palms and tree ferns, island laurels, juniper, even jacarandas from Brazil and the Australian paper tree.

All the islands are intensely cultivated with wheat, maize, beans, beetroot, tobacco, sweet potatoes, flax and tea. They also grow a wide variety of fruits—pineapples, bananas, passion fruit, oranges, strawberries, figs, apricots and loquats. And there are the flowers—great masses of pink and blue hydrangeas growing in hedgerows along the roads, as well as agapanthus, azaleas, camelias, roses, hibiscus, magnolias and acacias.

Animal life is similar to that of Europe, except that the Azores have no reptiles. There are numerous birds, especially seabirds. Buzzard hawks are common, and for centuries were mistaken for vultures—or, in Portuguese, *açores*—which caused the Portuguese discoverers to give this name to the islands. Game is abundant. The first settlers brought domestic animals, and livestock breeding is now one of the mainstays of the islands. There also is an abundance of fish, and deep sea fishing and underwater fishing are two of the major attractions to the islands. Cachalot, tunny, swordfish, mero, anchovy, barracuda and manta all frequent the seas off the Azores.

Climate

The Azores have a temperate, maritime climate. Winters are not severe, and summers are mild, with only slight changes in day-to-day temperatures. The climate, however, is damp. The islands get a lot of rain, and relative humidity is usually high, averaging between 75% and 77% for the year. The dampest month is January; the driest is March.

The average year-round temperature in the islands is 17° C. (62.6° F.). During August, temperatures average 22.3° C. (72.1° F.) and during February, temperatures average 14.3°C. (57.7° F.). Hail and frost are rare. In the winter, only the top of the island of Pico is covered with snow and ice.

The temperature of the sea is very close to that of the air—averaging between 17° C. and 24° C. (62.6° F. and 75.2° F.).

Afternoon cloudiness and rainfall are common throughout the year. Precipitation is highest from October to January. Rainfall then decreases through July, the month with the least precipitation. The less mountainous islands of Santa Maria, Graciosa and Corvo receive less rain than the others.

Winds are moderate and regular. Prevailing winds in the central and western groups of islands blow from the west and north. In the eastern group of islands, which are also situated more to the south, the northeast Trade Winds prevail for most of the year, except in winter when the Westerly blows in from the southwest. These southwesterly air masses are very damp and sometimes stormy, occasionally blowing at speeds up to 90 kilometers (56 miles) an hour. Average wind velocity in the Azores is 12.2 kilometers (7.6 miles) an hour.

Weather Forecasts

For most of the year, it is unnecessary to obtain forecasts before setting out on a walk. Just expect that it is going to cloud up and rain for a few hours in the afternoon. The tourist bureaus and hotel clerks can warn you about approaching storms if you ask. Storm warnings also are broadcast in Portuguese on the radio.

Where to Get Walking Information

You can obtain general tourist information on the Azores by writing its three tourist bureaus. But they can tell you little about walking on the islands. For details, you will have to wait until you are in the Azores and can visit the offices personally.

Delegação de Turismo de S. Miguel (for its address and telephone number, see the *Address Directory* at the back of this chapter). This is by far the most helpful of the three offices, and it can supply most of the maps and guidebooks listed in this chapter. You can write to the office in English, French, Spanish, German or Portuguese.

Delegação de Turismo da Terceira (see *Address Directory*). Provides information on the islands of Terceira, Graciosa and São Jorge. You can write in English, French, Spanish or Portuguese.

Delegação de Turismo do Faial (see *Address Directory*). Provides information on the islands of Faial, Pico, Flores and Corvo. Poor about responding to letters.

Branch offices of the *Centro de Turismo de Portugal* can also provide tourist information on the Azores.

Maps

Nine five-color maps in a scale of 1:50,000 and one map in a scale of 1:25,000 cover the Azores. They are published by:

Instituto Geográfico e Cadastral (see *Address Directory*). You can write in English, French, Spanish or Portuguese.

When ordering maps, you must ask for the *Arquipélago dos Açores* series. No index is available. Instead, you must order them by name:

- *Ilha de São Miguel (W), 1:50,000.* Covers the western half of the island. Last revision, 1971.
- *Ilha de São Miguel (E), 1:50,000.* Covers the eastern half of the island. Last revision, 1971.
- *Ilha de Santa Maria, 1:50,000.* Covers the island of Santa Maria. Last revision, 1965.
- *Ilha Terceira, 1:50,000.* Covers the island of Terceira. Last revision, 1965.
- *Ilha Graciosa, 1:50,000.* Covers the island of Graciosa. Last revision, 1968.
- *Ilha de São Jorge (W), 1:50,000.* Covers the western half of the island. Last revision, 1969.
- *Ilha de São Jorge (E), 1:50,000.* Covers the eastern half of the island. Last revision, 1969.
- *Ilha do Pico (E), 1:50,000.* Covers the eastern half of Pico. Last revision, 1969.

- *Ilha do Faial e do Pico (W), 1:50,000.* Covers the island of Faial and the western half of Pico. Last revision, 1969.
- *Ilhas das Flores e Corvo, 1:50,000.* Covers the two islands of Flores and Corvo. Last revision, 1969.
- *Ilha do Faial, 1:25,000.* Covers the island of Faial. Last updated in 1942.

Although the maps can be purchased in the Azores from the tourist offices, they carry only a small stock and do not have all the maps. To ensure you obtain the maps you need, it is best to order them by mail from the Instituto Geográfico. Also, be sure to allow at least six weeks to receive the maps.

Guidebooks

It is worth purchasing at least one of the tourist guides to the Azores. They provide a lot more information on the islands than the brochures available from the tourist offices. They also are useful in helping you plan your hikes since they note the areas of scenic and historic interest. Recommended guides include:

- *Açores,* Francisco Carreiro da Costa, Editorial de Publicações Turísticas, Lisbon, Portugal (see *Address Directory*). Written in Portuguese with French, English and German translations. Can be purchased from the tourist office on São Miguel.
- *Les Guides Bleus,* ed. Librarie Hachette, Paris. Available from most bookstores in Europe.

Trailside Lodgings

No trailside lodgings exist in the Azores. Hotels and pensions are located only in the major towns. In some towns, you also can stay in small, family-run boarding houses. Lists of the lodgings are available from the tourist offices.

Camping

Few restrictions exist on open camping. You can camp in any public field and on the shores of most lakes. Before camping on private property, you must ask the landowner's permission. If you don't, trespassing and vagrancy laws apply. Most uncultivated areas are open to public use. But just to be sure, check out your proposed campsites with the appropriate tourist office before you set out. They can tell you if one of the sites is on private property.

If you camp, you will have to carry your own provisions. They can be bought in every town.

There are no commercial campgrounds.

Water

There are many mineral springs scattered throughout the Azores. Some have a high content of sulfur and may have a distinct rotten egg smell. But you won't find a healthier source of water. Just check to be sure the spring is not hot before you drink.

Most streams and lakes are unpolluted, although you should not drink from those near animals or towns. Tap water throughout the Azores is safe.

Equipment Notes

In summer, light loose-fitting shirts and shorts are the most comfortable wear. For footwear, choose a pair of light full-grain leather boots that can be waterproofed. Sturdy walking shoes with vibram soles are adequate for forest paths, but should not be worn on mountain trails such as those on the island of Pico. In areas with dense undergrowth, long pants are recommended. A pair of cotton gloves to protect your hands from vines also is useful.

A windbreaker and raingear are essential. Also carry a light sweater.

In spring and winter, flannel or wool shirts should be worn, and a wool sweater should be carried in your pack.

During the rainy season and on low-lying forest paths during the summer, rubber boots are useful, as some trails may become quite muddy.

If you sleep out, you should carry a pestproof tent to keep rain and bugs out. Also, don't forget your insect repellent.

Guide Services

To explore the underground galleries and caves in the Azores requires a guide. One of the caves on the island of Graciosa—the Furna do Enxofre—includes an underground lake. Guides are also available for climbs up the steep, rocky slopes of 2,345 m (7,615 foot) Pico on the island by the same name. Information on hiring guides and on various guided excursions is available from the tourist offices.

Several travel agencies on the islands also can make arrangements for you to explore underground caves and to go deep sea fishing, hunting and scuba diving. Among these agencies, all located in São Miguel, are:

See *Address Directory*:

Agencia Açoreana de Viagens.
Agencia de Viagens e Turismo Ornelas.
Agencia de Viagens e Turismo Melo.
Agencia de Viagens Francisco C.S. Martins.
Agencia de Viagens Silva & Ferreira.
Pescatur Lda.

Search & Rescue

In case of an accident or emergency: On São Miguel, Terceira and Faial,call: Emergency Service: Tel. 115. On the other islands, call the police: Tel. 22022.

Transportation

Most of the islands have taxi and bus service between towns. On the island of São Miguel, rental cars are also available. On the island of Corvo, transportation is by donkey or by foot.

Among the islands of São Miguel, Santa Maria, Terceira, Faial and Flores there is regular air service on planes with 30 to 50 seats. There is also regular boat service between *all* of the islands.

Information on transport schedules and car rentals can be obtained from the tourist offices.

How to Get There

Several flights a week are made to the Azores by TAP airlines from Lisbon, New York and Montreal. Schedules and fares can be obtained by calling the airlines.

The Azores also can be reached by ship from Lisbon. Several sailings a month are made by the *Companhia Nacional de Navegação*. Information on the sailings can be obtained from any branch office of the Centro de Turismo de Portugal.

The Islands

Corvo

This is the smallest of the Azores—an island with an area of only 17 square kilometers (6.7 square miles). It has no high school, no doctors and its jail has not been occupied within memory. It has one small village with steep, narrow streets perched on the seacliffs. Its 450 residents have long devoted themselves to farming, grazing cattle and fishing on a semicommunal basis. In the interior of the island is the 776-meter (2,548-foot) high Monte Grosso, which overlooks the extinct Caldeirão crater, a lake with seven small islands. The crater can be reached on foot or by donkey.

Faial

Faial is one of the most inviting islands of the group. It has an area of 172 square kilometers (66.4 square miles) and a varied terrain. It often is called the "blue island" because of the abundance of hydrangeas growing along its narrow roads. The main town is Horta, built on rising ground above a beautiful bay. The western part of the island is volcanic. In 1957 a new volcano, Capelinhos, rose up from the sea and was active throughout 1958, adding a little to the island's total area. Inland is the 1042-meter (3,420-foot) volcano of Caldeira, an enchanting mountain surrounded by green meadowlands and lush vegetation. At the top, you look down into a crater, 1,850 meters (6,070 feet) in diameter and 400 meters (1,312 feet) in depth. The crater walls are covered with cedars, junipers, beeches, ferns and mosses. In the depths is a small, peaceful lake reflecting the green hues of the slopes around it. From the volcano there are wide views across the Atlantic to the islands of Pico, São Jorge, Terceira and Graciosa. For walking, there are many paths and back roads with little traffic, both along the coast and in the island's interior.

Flores

This island gets its name from its profusion of flowers. It is a veritable floating garden, exceeding all the other islands for greenery and the number of flowering hedgerows bordering its fields and pasturages. It has a rugged terrain with many lakes and waterfalls and a steep coastline honeycombed with caves. The main towns on the island are Santa Cruz and Lajes. It has an area of 142.8 square kilometers (55 square miles). Paths are short, but can be linked up by following mule tracks.

Graciosa

This is a relatively flat island of vineyards and cornfields dotted with Flemish-type windmills. It has an area of 60.8 square kilometers (23.5 square miles). In the interior of the island are the Caldeira hills and the Furna do Enxofre, a deep crater with an underground lake of warm, slightly sulphurous water. Sunlight streams through a narrow opening in the volcanic vault and glitters on the lake. The island also includes the Carapacho hot springs and the Serra das Fontes hills, where the peaks of Facho and Vimiais provide views out to the other islands.

Pico

Pico is separated from the island of Faial by a channel only 7 kilometers wide. Dominating the island is the mountain of Pico. At an altitude of 2,351 meters (7,713 feet), it is the highest point in the Azores—and higher than any point on Portuguese territory. The rest of the island is covered with forests of chestnut and pine trees, great expanses of black lava, vineyards and fig-groves. At Santa Luzia there is an almost completely bare expanse of lava, with many outcrops that cooled into strange shapes, known locally as *mistérios*. There also are the Frei Matias caves with stalactites and the Caldeira, a 30-meter (99-foot) deep crater. In its center is a 70-meter (230-foot) volcanic cone with steaming fumaroles. The coastline of the island has steep lava cliffs and many secluded inlets. The area of the island is 433.2 square kilometers (167 square miles). It is a good island to explore by foot.

Santa Maria

This island boasts many large bays and beaches of soft golden sand. The southernmost island in the archipelago, it was the first to be discovered. Its main town, Vila do Porto, was the first township in the Azores and still preserves many traditions of Portugal from the mid-15th century. The island is dotted with old pottery kilns, as well as ruins dating from the 15th and 16th centuries. At Santa Ana there is a limestone deposit with marine fossils. There are many churches, well-enclosed vineyards and windmills. The international airport linking the Azores to Lisbon and North America is located on the island. Near the island is the Romeiro Islet, which has a cave with stalactites, and the Formigas Islets, a fully protected nature reserve. The area of the island is 97 square kilometers (37.4 square miles).

São Jorge

A long, narrow island ringed by steep cliffs that plunge to the sea, São Jorge is known as the "Switzerland of the Azores." It is 65 kilometers (40 miles) long and, in some places, no more than four kilometers (2.5 miles) wide. It is an island of wide, green pastures separated by hedges of hydrangeas and cedars. Cyprus woods dot the island. Among the high cliffs there are many waterfalls and, down near the shore, the characteristic *fajás*—tongues of land—with their white-washed houses half hidden among vines and orchards. By following roads part of the way, it is possible to walk the length of the island. Cliff paths lead down to the *fajás*.

São Miguel

This is the largest and most important island of the archipelago. It has a rugged coastline with many inlets and is covered with lush, semi-tropical vegetation. There are several hot springs, geysers and lakes scattered across the island. The town of Ponta Delgada, with its many old churches, palaces and mansions, is the largest in the Azores. At Sete Cidades there is a gigantic extinct crater with an area of 40 square kilometers. At the bottom is a verdant valley with a village and two lakes, one blue, the other green. According to legend, one of the seven cities of Atlantis was submerged in this crater. The Vale das Furnas is the best known part of the Azores and one of its richest spas. It is a deep volcanic valley covered with luxuriant vegetation, tea plantations and tree-shaded paths. Inside the valley is the Terra Nostra Park, one of the most complete botanical gardens in Europe. From here, there are many walks up to the surrounding peaks: Pico do Salto do Cavalo, Gafanhoto, Ferro and Ribeira da Água Quente. Total area of the island is 2,304.5 square kilometers (890 square miles). Along with Pico and Terceira this is one of the best islands in the Azores on which to walk.

Terceira

During the 16th, 17th and 18th centuries this island played an important role in Portuguese history. It also was an important port for ships sailing between India and Brazil. To the north lie the Quatro Ribeiras Hills, accessible along forest paths, and the strangely beautiful country around Biscoitos where the vineyards grow between volcanic walls. Surrounding the pastures are sheets of lava and volcanic cones, which give a moon-like effect to the area. From the Caldeira de Santa Bárbara, 1,023 meters (3,356 feet) high, the islands of São Jorge and Graciosa can be seen. There also are several caves and underground galleries that can be explored with a guide. Area of the island is 396.8 square kilometers (153 square miles). Footpaths are numerous, though short.

Address Directory

A

- *Agencia Acoreana de Viagens,* Lado Sul da Matriz, Ponta Delgada, São Miguel, Azores. Tel. 25397.
- *Agencia de Viagens e Turismo Melo,* Rua de Santa Luzia, Ponta Delgada, São Miguel, Azores. Tel. 25314.
- *Agencia de Viagens e Turismo Ornelas,* Avenida Infante D. Henrique, Ponta Delgada, São Miguel, Azores. Tel. 22236.
- *Agencia de Viagens Francisco C.S. Martins,* Rua Marquês Praia Monforte, Ponta Delgada, São Miguel, Azores. Tel. 22094.
- *Agencia de Viagens Silva & Ferreira,* Rua Hintze Ribeiro, Ponta Delgada, São Miguel, Azores. Tel. 24791.

D

- *Delegação de Turismo do Faial,* Rua Conselhuiro Medeiros, Horta, Faial, Azores. Tel. 22237.
- *Delegação de Turismo da Terceira,* Rua de Lisboa, Angra do Heroismo, Terceira, Azores. Tel. 23141.
- *Delegação de Turismo de S. Miguel* Avenida Infante D. Henrique, Ponta Delgada, São Miguel, Azores. Tel. 25743.

E

- *Editoral de Publicacões Turísticas,* R. de Santa Bárbara, 81 5.ᐧ-D, Lisboa-1, Portugal.
- *Emergency:* São Miguel, Terceira and Faial, Tel. 115. Other islands, call police, Tel. 22022.

I

- *Instituto Geográfico e Cadastral,* Venda de Cartas, Praça da Estrela, Lisboa-2, Portugal.

P

- *Pescatur, Lda.* Rua José M. R. Amaral, Ponta Delgada, São Miguel, Azores. Tel. 22827.

A Quick Reference

In a hurry? Turn to the pages listed below. They will give you the most important information on walking in the Azores.

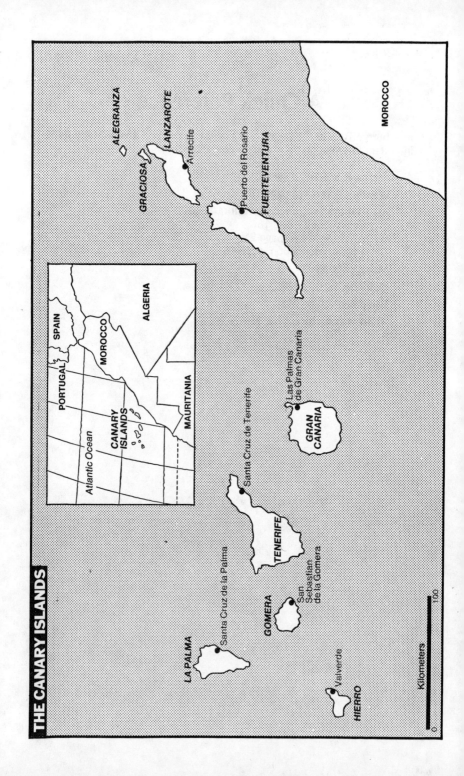

THE CANARY ISLANDS

The Canary Islands

THE CANARY ISLANDS LIE in the North Atlantic off the west coast of Africa. They consist of seven islands and six islets, covering a total of 7,273 square kilometers (2,808 square miles). The high western islands—Tenerife, Gran Canaria, La Palma, Gomera and Hierro—are the tips of volcanoes that rise from the ocean floor. All are characterized by steep, rugged mountains, the highest of which is 3,718-meter (12,198-foot) Pico del Teide on the island of Tenerife.

The lower eastern islands—Lanzarote, Fuerteventura and the six islets nearby—all surmount a single undersea plateau, which rises some 1,372 meters (4,500 feet) from the ocean floor. It too, like the high western islands, is of volcanic origin. All the islands are volcanic ejection cones built up from eruptions that occurred millions of years ago. Large eruptions, however, occurred from vents on Lanzarote as recently as the 18th and 19th centuries.

The Canary Islands are best known for their mild year-round climate and beautiful sandy beaches, which have the usual complement of resort hotels and other tourist facilities. But they also offer excellent walking opportunities. Of particular note is the wide variety of terrain and vegetation that exists only short distances apart on the same island. In a single day you can traverse snowfields or roam along warm, sandy beaches; walk through pine forests or through subtropical plantations of coffee, bananas and sugarcane. Footpaths lead to deserted coasts, follow ridge tops with spectacular views of neighboring islands and the Atlantic, climb through cool mountain forests, descend into giant craters and cross volcanic wastelands littered with cinder cones.

Although spring is the best time to walk in the mountains, any time of year is good. And if you are not equipped to face the snow and cold of Pico de Teide during the winter, you can walk instead in the balmy lowlands. Conversely, if the summer heat becomes oppressive along the coast, you need only climb the mountains to escape it. Footpaths exist on all the islands, and some of the routes—such as those on Tenerife—are signposted at the points where they strike off from roads and villages. None of the paths are marked enroute, however; and while many are clearly defined, there are exceptions. Hence, it is advisable to obtain the appropriate topographical maps before you venture up the paths.

The Canary Islands comprise two of Spain's provinces—that of Santa

Cruz de Tenerife, which includes Tenerife, La Palma, Gomera and Hierro; and of Las Palmas, which includes Gran Canaria, Lanzarote, Fuerteventura and their neighboring islets. Spanish (Castilian) is the official language, although French, English and German are spoken by those connected with the tourist industry in the larger towns. Some walking information—what little of it exists—is also translated into French, English and German.

Flora & Fauna

The vegetation of the Canary Islands is highly varied, ranging from luxuriant subtropical forest to desert scrub. This variety results from the profound effect the mountains have on local climates. The windward slopes, which face north and east, receive the most rain and consequently have the densest vegetation. The southern and western sides of the islands lie in the rainshadow of the peaks and are typically desertlike.

Rainfall also increases with elevation and changes in vegetation are apparent as you climb from the coast to the mountaintops. Below 396 meters (1,300 feet), the climate is like that of Egypt. Desert plants thrive in this zone, and the main crops are bananas, oranges, coffee, dates, sugarcane and tobacco. From 396 to 732 meters (1,300 to 2,400 feet), the climate is somewhat drier and cooler—more like that of southern Italy— and the main crops are cereals, grapes and potatoes. From 732 to 1,219 meters (2,400 to 4,000 feet), the most common vegetation is a mixture of scrub and open woodland in which holly, myrtle and laurel are the most conspicuous plants. Above 1,219 meters, woodlands dominated by Canary Island pine and tree heaths mingle with areas of scrub and grassland.

It is expressly forbidden to pick or otherwise disturb plants in the Parque Nacional del Teide on Tenerife or in the Parque Nacional de la Caldera de Taburiente on La Palma.

Wild animals include lizards, rabbits, field mice and rats, as well as a few hedgehogs. Numerous birds inhabit the island, including goldcrests, woodpeckers, tits, warblers, owls, seabirds and several finches, including that renowned singer the canary. There are no venomous snakes and only a few mosquitoes, which breed in ponds during the summer.

Climate

The mild subtropical climate of the Canary Islands is moderated by the surrounding sea and the northeast trade winds. Seasonal changes are slight, with average summer and winter temperatures only a few degrees apart. Daytime temperatures during the winter normally range between

15° and 20° C. (59° to 68° F.) and during the summer, between 20° and 28° C. (68° to 82.4° F.). January temperatures at sea level sometimes reach 25° C. or slightly more during the day and seldom fall below 10° C. at night. Summer temperatures at sea level can rise to as high as 37° to 40° C. on the hottest days, but are usually much cooler. In other words, the Canary Islands enjoy a balmy springlike climate the year round.

The greatest difference among the seasons is in the amounts of rainfall received. Most precipitation falls during the winter. Lesser amounts are received during spring and fall, and rainfall in the summer months is negligible. The amount of rain received from place to place is highly variable, depending on elevation and location with respect to the mountains. The coastal town of Puerto de la Cruz, for example, situated on the windward side of Tenerife, receives an average of 408.8 mm (16 inches) of rain per year, while Santa Cruz de Tenerife, also at sea level but on the leeward side of the island, receives an annual average of only 243.8 mm (9.6 inches) of rain.

The mountains, however, receive from six to nine times as much precipitation as the coast, and above 2,000 meters, snow covers the slopes during the winter. The first snowfall of the year sometimes mantles the slopes of Pico del Teide as early as November, but may melt shortly after falling. Snow usually remains on the upper slopes from December through March, and as late as April in cool years. There is not enough snow, however, for skiing.

Winter storms arrive from the northeast, borne by the tradewinds, but seldom occur more than two or three times a month and usually last only 36 to 48 hours. Overcast skies occur only about four days a month during the winter and not at all during the summer, although scattered clouds often form over the mountains on summer afternoons.

Weather Forecasts

During the summer months, when days are always sunny and warm, you will not need a weather forecast. But the rest of the year, when storms are possible, you would do well to obtain a forecast before setting out into the mountains. You can obtain a recorded forecast in Spanish by telephoning:

Centro Meteorológico de Canarias Occidentale: Tel. (922) 21 17 18.

Where to Get Walking Information

There are two walking clubs in the Canary Islands, both of which are provincial sections of the Federación Español de Montañismo (F.E.M.) in Madrid. Both clubs can give you details about walking in their provinces. Unfortunately, neither club is good about answering written enquiries, even in Spanish. Consequently, you may have to wait until you are in the Canaries and can visit them in person. But this is the clubs' only failing. In person, the club members are gregarious, go out of their way to help foreign walkers, and once in awhile, even invite you to join in club activities. The clubs are:

Federación Canaria de Montañismo (for its address, see the *Address Directory* at the back of this chapter). Affiliated with seven local clubs devoted to mountaineering.

Federación Tinefeña de Montañismo (see *Address Directory*). Affiliated with 10 local clubs devoted to mountaineering.

As an alternative to writing the walking clubs, you can try writing the tourist offices. In addition to lodging lists, brochures on the Canary Islands and cther tourist information, several of the offices can provide information on walking—perhaps not quite as complete as that which you can get from the walking clubs, but at least you are more likely to get an answer. The provincial tourist office on Santa Cruz de Tenerife is the best about answering enquiries on walking. It can also provide a series of sketch maps to paths on the island (see the section on *Maps*). The tourist offices are:

See *Address Directory*:

Ministerio de Transporte, Turismo y Comunicaciones Santa Cruz de Tenerife. Provides information on the islands of Gomero, Hierro, La Palma and Tenerife. Staff speaks Spanish, French, English and German. Very helpful.

Ministerio de Transporte, Turismo y Comunicaciones Las Palmas de Gran Canaria. Provides information on the islands of Gran Canaria, Feurteventura and Lanzarote. Staff speaks Spanish, English and French.

Oficina de Turismo, Santa Cruz de Tenerife. Provides information on the island of Tenerife and the city of Santa Cruz de Tenerife. Staff speaks Spanish, French, English and German.

Oficina de Turismo, Puerto de la Cruz. Provides information on the region surrounding Puerto de la Cruz on the northern coast of Tenerife. Staff speaks Spanish, French and English.

Oficina de Turismo, Las Palmas de Gran Canaria. Provides information on the islands of Gran Canaria Lanzarote and Fuerteventura, and on the city of Las Palmas de Gran Canaria. Staff speaks Spanish, French and English.

Maps

Forty-three topographical sheets in a scale of 1:50,000 cover the Canary Islands. They are published by the:

Instituto Geográfico y Catastral (see *Address Directory*). Located in Madrid, Spain. Staff speaks Spanish and French.

The maps, an index and price list can be obtained by mail from the I.G.C. When ordering, specify the name and sheet number of each map you need.

You can also obtain the maps once you are in the Canary Islands from:

Servicio Geográfico de Ejercito (see *Address Directory*).

Sketch Maps

If you plan to walk on the island of Tenerife, you should obtain the series of walkers' sketch maps published by ICONA—the Instituto Nacional Conservación de la Naturaleza—in collaboration with the Cabildo Insular de Tenerife, the island's ruling council. Each of the 10 maps in the series covers one of 10 zones into which the island has been divided. The maps show all the footpaths in each zone and indicate those that are steep or rough. The paths are posted with signs reading *Sendero touristico*. The maps also show roads, forest tracks, trailside shelters (for day use only), rest areas, picnic areas, parking places and viewpoints. A legend explains the map symbols in Spanish, French, German and English. The maps can be obtained for a nominal charge from tourist offices on the island of Tenerife or from:

Jefaturas Regionales de ICONA in Santa Cruz de Tenerife (see *Address Directory*).

A similar series of sketch maps is also available for the island of Gran Canaria. Information on these maps can be obtained from:

Jefaturas Regionales de ICONA in Las Palmas Gran Canaria (see *Address Directory*).

The bus line servicing the island of Gran Canaria publishes a route schedule that includes a sketch map of the island on which footpaths are indicated by dashed lines. Although this map is not suitable for use on the trail, it does suggest numerous walking possibilities. You can obtain the bus schedule and map from:

> **Salcai** (see *Address Directory*).

Guidebooks

At present there are no guidebooks to the footpaths of the Canary Islands. You will have to rely on whatever maps are available to find your way. There is little danger of getting lost, however, for most paths are short and you can always orient yourself by means of the sea, which is frequently in view. Nevertheless, you should always carry the appropriate topographical maps and an orienteering compass when following mountain paths.

Trailside Lodgings

There is only one trailside refuge open to the public in all of the Canary Islands—the Refugio de Altavista. It is located high on the northeast slope of Pico de Teide on the island of Tenerife and can accommodate as many as 20 people at a time. The refuge is maintained by the island council:

> **El Cabildo Insular de Tenerife** (see *Address Directory*).

A second refuge is located in the mountains of Tenerife at Azulejoz, but it may be used only by members of the Federación Español de Montañismo and affiliated clubs.

The Ministerio de Información y Turismo operates five national tourist inns, which offer complete hotel facilities. Two of these inns are of particular interest to walkers: the one at Cruz de Tejeda on Gran Canaria and the one at Las Cañadas del Teide on Tenerife. Each is located in the heart of a prime walking region. For information on national tourist inns, as well as other accommodation, contact the local tourist offices.

Camping

Since most walking regions in the Canaries lack hotels and refuges, it will be necessary to camp if you intend to take extended walks. Although there are no organized campgrounds, camping is permitted in many places throughout the islands. If you wish to camp near a town, you should first obtain permission from the local authorities at the nearest town hall. Permission to camp in other areas should first be obtained from the Gobierno Civil—the local police—on each island or from ICONA (see *Address Directory*).

Water

It is advisable to carry plenty of water when walking anywhere in the Canary Islands. It is safe to drink from springs and year-round streams in the mountains, but they are very few in number. Standing water should be avoided. Tap water, however, is safe to drink.

Equipment Notes

Light, loose-fitting shirts and shorts are the most comfortable clothing for summer walking, although you should also take a windbreaker if you plan to walk at high altitudes. The best footwear for the islands sometimes rocky terrain is a pair of lightweight, but sturdy, hiking boots. In addition to a good supply of water, you should take some salt tablets; a wide-brim hat is also advised. Camping equipment will be necessary for extended walks. You should also carry a compass and the appropriate topographical maps.

In spring and fall, when occasional rainstorms visit the islands, you will need raingear and warmer clothing. If you plan to walk in the mountains during the winter, you will also need a warm parka, lined boots, wool clothing (including cap and gloves), gaiters, an ice axe and crampons for crossing icy slopes and equipment for cold-weather camping. Above 2,000 meters, appropriate snow gear will be necessary from November through April.

If you plan to camp out, be sure to carry a stove, for firewood is scarce over much of the islands. A tent is optional during the summer, but advisable the rest of the year.

Transportation

Most of the islands have taxi and bus service. There is both air and boat service between the islands. For information on fares and schedules, contact the local tourist offices (see *Address Directory*).

How to Get There

Regular scheduled flights link the Canary Islands with Europe, America and the west coast of Africa. Direct flights from Madrid on Iberia Airlines take just over two hours. The islands are also visited by many of the ocean liners plying this region of the Atlantic. For information, contact your travel agent.

Useful Addresses & Telephone Numbers

General Tourist Information

In the Canaries:

See the list of local tourist offices under the section on *Where to Get Walking Information*.

Abroad:

Information on the Canary Islands can be obtained from branch offices of the Spanish National Tourist Office in EUROPE: Brussels, Copenhagen, Düsseldorf, Frankfurt, Geneva, Hamburg, Helsinki, The Hague, Lisbon, London, Milan, Munich, Oslo, Paris, Rome, Stockholm, Vienna and Zurich; JAPAN: Tokyo; CANADA: Toronto; and the U.S.A.: Chicago, San Francisco, Houston, St. Augustine and New York.

London: Spanish National Tourist Office, 57-58 St. James Street, London SW1A 1LD. Tel. (01) 499 1095.

New York: Spanish National Tourist Office, 665 Fifth Avenue, New York, New York 10022. Tel. (212) 759-8822.

Sport Shops

A limited selection of walking and mountaineering equipment can be obtained from the following sport shops in Santa Cruz de Tenerife:

See *Address Directory*:

Manuel Lovero Morro
Galerías Deportivas
Deportes Guerra
Deportes Mario
Golden Star

Search & Rescue

In an emergency: Find the nearest telephone and contact the Guardia Civil. The telephone numbers to call on each island are as follows:
Fuerteventura: Tel. 85 05 03.
Gran Canaria: Tel. 21 58 17.
Gomera: Tel. 87 02 55.
Hierro: Tel. 55 01 05.
Lanzarote: Tel. 81 09 46.
La Palma: Tel. 41 11 84.
Tenerife: Tel. 22 31 00.

Search and rescue operations in the Canary Islands are carried out by the Guardia Civil—the provincial police—in conjunction with volunteers from the islands' various mountaineering groups. There is no charge for the search and rescue operations, although in some cases you may have to pay transportation costs if a helicopter or ambulance is required for evacuation. You will also be responsible for medical costs.

The Islands

Fuerteventura

Fuerteventura, the second largest of the Canary Islands, covers 2,019 square kilometers (779 square miles). It lies southwest of Lanzarote. The island is roughly elliptical in shape except for a triangular peninsula on the south end, which is connected to the remainder of the island by a narrow isthmus. A low ridge runs from north to south the length of the island. The highest point on the ridge is 593-meter (1,946-foot) Rosa del Taro. The western side of the island is mostly deserted. Walks are possible both in the mountains and along the coast, which boasts some of the finest beaches in the islands.

Maps:
* I.G.C. Mapa Nacional Topografico 1:50,000, sheets 1.092 *Cotillo*, 1.093 *Lobos*, 1.098 *La Oliva*, 1.099 *Puerto de Lajas*, 1.106 *Puerto de Cabras*, 1.114 *Istmo de la Pared*, 1.115 *Tuineje* and 1.122 *Jandía*.

Gran Canaria

This is the third largest of the Canary Islands, covering 1,532 square kilometers (591 square miles). The city of Las Palmas, with about 300,000 inhabitants, is the largest on the island and capital of the province which includes the islands of Gran Canaria, Lanzarote and Fuerteventura. Located due east of Tenerife, Gran Canaria is noted for its climatic and vegetational extremes. The windward half of the island, which lies north of the central mountain massif, receives ample rainfall and supports pine forests as well as plantations devoted to growing grapes, coffee, palms, bananas, almonds, sugar cane and tomatoes. The southern half of the island is extremely arid, particularly near Maspalomas, which has extensive sand dunes. Roque Nublo, the granite crest of the island, is more than 1,981 meters (6,500 feet) high. Numerous footpaths lead through the mountains, across the southern desert and down to deserted sections of the coast.

Maps:
* I.G.C. Mapa Nacional Topografico 1:50,000, sheets 1.113 *La Isleta*, 1.120 *Punta de Guanarteme y Arucas*, 1.121 *Las Palmas de Gran Canaria*, 1.125 *San Nicolás de Tolentino*, 1.126 *Ingenio*, 1.128 *Maspalomas* and 1.129 *Juan Grande*.

Gomera

The round, green island of Gomera covers 378 square kilometers (146 square miles). Rising in the center of the island is 1,487-meter (4,878-foot) Alto de Garajonay. The coastline is steep and rocky. Walks are possible both in the mountains and along stretches of uninhabited coast. Gomera plays an important role in history, for it is there that Columbus refitted his ships before sailing west to the Americas.

Maps:
• I.G.C. Mapa Nacional Topografico 1:50,000, sheets 1.108 *Vallehermoso,* 1.109 *Los Carrizales y Agulo,* 1.116 *Valle Gran Rey* and 1.117 *San Sebastián de la Gomera.*

Hierro

Smallest and westernmost of the main Canary Islands, Hierro covers only 278 square kilometers (107 square miles). The island's central plateau reaches its greatest height at Mal Paso (1,501 meters; 4,924 feet). The fertile soils support extensive woodlands of beech and pine, which in places extend to the edge of the sea. Most of the coastline is steep and rocky. Several walks are possible in the mountains and along the coast.

Maps:
• I.G.C. Mapa Nacional Topografico 1:50,000, sheets 1.127 *Valverde* and 1.130 *La Restinga.*

Lanzarote

The most recent volcanic activity in the Canary Islands occurred during the 18th and 19th centuries on the island of Lanzarote, which lies only 111 kilometers (69 miles) from the west coast of Africa. Great eruptions spewed tons of volcanic ash and lava over the island, completely transforming its appearance. Today, much of the island is a volcanic wasteland of colorful cinder cones and vast expanses of ash and pumice. Volcanic fires can still be seen a few meters below the surface on the Montaña del Fuego ("Mountain of Fire"), on the west side of the island. Numerous walking possibilities exist.

Maps:
• I.G.C. Mapa Nacional Topografico 1:50,000, sheets 1.082 Graciosa, 1.083 Teguise, 1.084 Haría, 1.087 Pechiguera, 1.088 Arrecife and 1.089 El Charco.

La Palma

Known as the "pretty isle," La Palma lies a few kilometers northwest of Tenerife and covers 728 square kilometers (281 square miles). The land rises steeply from the sea to the summit of Roque de los Muchachos (2,437 meters; 7,996 feet) on the rim of the yawning Caldera de Taburiente, encompassed within a national park. La Palma is said to have the greatest elevation for its circumference of any island in the world. The summit caldera, vying in size with that of Haleakala in Hawaii, is almost 27 kilometers in circumference and as much as 774 meters (2,540 feet) deep. The upper flanks of the caldera support extensive pine groves. You can walk either around the rim of the crater or into its depths. Walks are also possible in the mountains extending south from the caldera.

Maps:
- I.G.C. Mapa Nacional Topografico 1:50,000, sheets 1.085 *San Andrés y los Sauces,* 1.090 *Santa Cruz de la Palma* and 1.094 *Fuencaliente de la Palma.*

Tenerife

This is the largest of the Canary Islands, covering 3,199 square kilometers (1,235 square miles). Santa Cruz de Tenerife, a city of about 200,000 inhabitants, is the capital of the province which includes the islands of Tenerife, La Palma, Gomero and Hierro. The mountain range forming the spine of this triangular island culminates in 3,718-meter (12,198-foot) Pico de Teide, the highest point in the Canaries. To the south lies the gigantic crater of Las Cañadas del Teide, which lies within a national park. Fertile valleys run down both sides of the mountain backbone, those of Orotava and Güimar being the most notable. The coast is alternately gentle and rugged, with both steep cliffs and beaches of black or golden sand. Numerous footpaths wander through the valleys and into the mountains. Sketch maps showing these paths are available from the island's tourist offices (see *Address Directory*).

Maps:
- I.G.C. Mapa Nacional Topografico 1:50,000, sheets 1.096 *Teguesta,* 1.097 *Punta de Anaga,* 1.102 *Punta de Teno,* 1.103 *Icod de los Vinos,* 1.104 *Santa Cruz de Tenerife y San Andrés,* 1.109 *Los Carrizales y Aguolo,* 1.110 *Guía de Isora,* 1.111 *Guimar,* 1.118 *Granadilla de Abona y las Galletas* and 1.119 *Lomo de Arico.*
- *Tenerife: sendero turistico,* Cabildo/ICONA, sheets Zona 1, Zona 2, Zona 3, Zona 4, Zona 5, Zona 6, Zona 7, Zona 8, Zona 9 and Zona 10.

Address Directory

D

- *Deportes Guerra,* Avenida La Salle 4, Santa Cruz de Tenerife. Tel. (922) 22 83 44.
- *Deportes Mario,* San Sebastián 98, Santa Cruz de Tenerife. Tel. (922) 21 12 61.

E

- *El Cabildo Insular de Tenerife,* Plaza de España Santa Cruz de Tenerife. Tel. (922) 24 20 90.
- *Emergency:* Find the nearest telephone and contact the Guardia Civil. The telephone numbers to call on each island are as follows: Fuerteventura: Tel. 85 05 03; Gran Canaria: Tel. 21 58 17; Gomera: Tel. 87 02 55; Hierro: Tel. 55 01 05; Lanzarote: Tel. 81 09 46; La Palma: Tel. 41 11 84; and Tenerife: Tel. 22 31 00.

F

- *Federación Canaria de Montañismo,* La Naval 32, Las Palmas de Gran Canaria.
- *Federación Tinefena de Montañismo,* San Sebastián 76, Santa Cruz de Tenerife. Tel. (922) 24 20 44.

G

- *Galerias Deportivas,* Villalba Hervás 6, Santa Cruz de Tenerife. Tel. (922) 24 24 01.
- *Golden Star,* General Franco 6, Santa Cruz de Tenerife. Tel. (922) 27 30 61.

I

- *ICONA,* see *Jefaturas Regionales de ICONA.*
- *Instituto Geográfico y Catastral,* Calle General Ibáñez de Ibero 3, Madrid 3, Spain. Tel. (91) 234 51 16.

J

- *Jefaturas Regionales de ICONA, Las Palmas,* Canarias Orientales, Distrito Forestal, Tina 104, Las Palmas de Gran Canaria. Tel. (928) 54 79.

- *Jefaturas Regionales de ICONA, Santa Cruz,* Canarıas Occidentales, Distrito Forestal, Castillo 8, Santa Cruz de Tenerife. Tel. (922) 17 16 or 60 80.

M

- *Manuel Lovero Morro,* Imeldo Seris 47, Santa Cruz de Tenerife. Tel. (922) 24 57 62 or 24 69 73.

- *Ministerio de Transporte, Turismo y Comunicaciones Las Palmas,* Delegación Provincial, Calle de Triana 60, Las Palmas de Gran Canaria. Tel. (928) 21 54 31 or 21 50 93.

- *Ministerio de Transporte, Turismo y Comunicaciones Santa Cruz,* Delegación Provincial, Calle de la Marina 57, Santa Cruz de Tenerife. Tel. (922) 28 21 58 or 28 21 00.

O

- *Oficina de Turismo, Las Palmas,* Casa del Turismo, Parque Santa Catalina, Las Palmas de Gran Canaria. Tel. (928) 26 46 23.

- *Oficina de Turismo, Puerto de la Cruz,* Plaza de la Iglesia, Puerto de la Cruz. Tel. (922) 27 19 28.

- *Oficina de Turismo, Santa Cruz,* Plaza de Espana Edificio de Cabildo Insular, Santa Cruz de Tenerife. Tel. (922) 24 22 27.

- *Oficina del Patronato Insular de Turismo,* Avenida José Antonio, Edificio del Cabildo Insular, Santa Cruz de Tenerife. Tel. (922) 24 20 90.

S

- *Salcai,* Oficinas Centrales, Viera y Calvijo 34 y 36, Las Palmas de Gran Canaria.

- *Servicio Geográfico de Ejercito,* Rambla 25 de Julio, Santa Cruz de Tenerife.

- *Spanish National Tourist Office, London,* 57-58 St. James Street, London SW1A 1LD. Tel. (01) 499 1095.

- *Spanish National Tourist Office, New York,* 665 Fifth Avenue, New York, New York 10022. Tel. (212) 759-8822.

W

- *Weather:* Centro Meteorologico de Canarias Occidentale: Tel. (922) 21 17 18.

A Quick Reference

In a hurry? Turn to the pages listed below. They will give you the most important information on walking in the Canary Islands.

MADEIRA'S FOOTPATHS

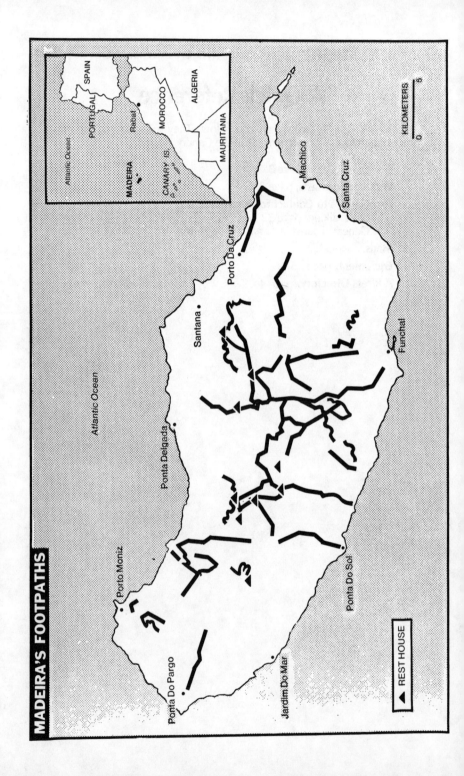

▲ REST HOUSE

KILOMETERS
0   5

Porto Moniz

Ponta Do Pargo

Jardim Do Mar

Ponta Do Sol

Ponta Delgada

Atlantic Ocean

Santana

Porto Da Cruz

Machico

Santa Cruz

Funchal

Atlantic Ocean

PORTUGAL

SPAIN

Rabat

MOROCCO

ALGERIA

MAURITANIA

MADEIRA

CANARY IS.

Madeira

THE PORTUGUESE ISLAND of Madeira lies in the North Atlantic 978 kilometers (607 miles) southwest of Lisbon and 545 kilometers (339 miles) west of Cabo Djouchi on the west coast of Africa. It is a lush garden isle famous for its resorts, but which also offers splendid walking in the mountains of the interior. Although the peaks are not particularly lofty—the highest being Pico Ruivo at 1,861 meters (6,106 feet)—they are extremely rugged, with steep flanks plunging to river gorges, and sharp pinnacles and crags crowning the highest ridges. The mountains are largely uninhabited, and numerous well-marked footpaths of all degrees of difficuty lead through lush forests, along mountain streams, near water-falls and to the summits of the highest peaks.

Madeira is only 57 kilometers (35 miles) long and 22 kilometers (14 miles) wide, covering an area of 741 square kilometers (286 square miles). About 300,000 people live on the island, a third of them in the capital city of Funchal, on the southern coast. Agriculture is still a mainstay of the Madeiran economy, and traditional farming communities are found—as they have been for centuries—at the mouths of mountain canyons.

Madeira and the nearby Funchal Islands—largest of which is Porto Santo (42 square kilometers; 16 square miles)—are the exposed summits of a chain of submarine volcanoes. The remainder of the chain consists of small, deserted islets. Port Santo has some 3,000 residents, most of whom are involved in growing grapes, cereals, figs, melons and other fruits. Walking possibilities on the Funchal Islands, however, are strictly limited.

Flora & Fauna

Madeira is a lush, verdant island whose mountains are densely clothed with forests of pine and a wide variety of broadleaved trees, many of which were imported from other parts of the world—eucalyptus, acacia, jacaranda and several types of tropical fruit trees, for instance. Steep slopes where the soil is too thin to support trees are often covered with grasses and shrubs. The Paúl da Serra plateau, on the western half of the island, is largely given over to moors.

Flowers seem to be everywhere. Native forget-me-nots, orchids, fox-gloves, hydrangeas and arum lilies carpet the forest floor. The bird of paradise, bougainvillea, flamingo flower and numerous other exotic species grow throughout much of the island.

The chief crops are bananas, sugarcane and grapes. From the island's vineyards come the grapes that make the famous Madeira wines, which have been drunk in England since Elizabethan times. Other commercially grown fruits include mango, papaya, avocado and passion fruit. Vegetables and flowers are also grown as crops.

Although the island's volcanic soils are fertile, the steep terrain made agriculture difficult for Madeira's early settlers. They solved the problem by terracing the steep slopes of the canyons and by constructing a series of irrigation canals—or *levadas*—to bring water from the mountains to the terraced gardens. This system is still in use today, and farming villages nestled among terraced slopes at the mouths of the canyons are familiar and characteristic scenes in the Madeiran landscape. Many of the island's footpaths follow the levadas in their gently winding courses down the mountains.

The most common wild mammals on the island are rabbits and feral goats. There are, also, many species of land and seabirds that inhabit the forests and rocky shores. Trout, which were introduced to the island, thrive in most mountain streams. Offshore game fish include amberjack, blue marlin, swordfish and several large species of shark.

Climate

Madeira's climate is warm and mostly sunny all year long. The average temperature is 16°C. (61°F.) during the winter and 21°C. (70°F.) during the summer. The temperature of the ocean closely follows that of the land, dropping below it only from mid-August through November. September is the hottest month; February the coldest. Most rains fall during the winter. Snow is unknown, even at higher elevations. The mountains, however, tend to be cooler and moister than the coastal areas, enough so that a sweater may be required at high elevations during the summer. The peaks can also be suddenly obscured by dense mists that can make navigation difficult. You may walk in the mountains throughout the year.

Weather Forecasts

Weather forecasts can be obtained from the tourist office in Funchal (see below). In addition, many hall porters in the major hotels can tell you what weather conditions are likely to be.

Where to Get Walking Information

You can obtain walking information from:

Direcção Regional de Turismo (for its address and telephone number, see the *Address Directory* at the back of this chapter). Staff speaks Portuguese, Spanish, French and English. The tourist association publishes the only guidebook to footpaths in all of Portugal. It also publishes a map showing footpaths on the island. Both are listed below.

There are no walking clubs on Madeira.

Maps

Two topographical maps in a scale of 1:50,000 cover the island of Madeira. They are published by:

Instituto Geográfico e Cadastral (see *Address Directory*). You may write in English, French, Spanish or Portuguese.

When ordering maps, you must ask for the *Arquipélago da Madeira, Ilha da Madeira (W)* and *Ilha da Madeira (E)*. The maps show roads, footpaths and levadas, as well as different types of vegetation. Topographical relief is indicated by contour lines.

Another 1:100,000 map covering the entire island is published by the Direcção Regional de Turismo. The map, entitled simply *Madeira*, shows the principal footpaths on the island as black dashes. The locations of government rest houses, streams and rivers, the elevations of peaks, villages and roads are shown, as well as the road distances between locals. Topographical relief on the map is approximated by shading. On the flip side is a street map of the town of Funchal. The map is not suitable for use on the trail, but it provides much useful information to help you plan walks using the tourist association's guidebook and the appropriate 1:50,000 topographical maps.

Guidebooks

A single guidebook covers the principal footpaths of Madeira:

- *Walks, Promenades, Spaziergänge, Passeios a Pé: Madeira* (in English, French, German and Portuguese). Published by the Direcção Regional de Turismo. Covers 16 walks, each illustrated by a color photograph and sketch map. Symbols indicate degree of difficulty, locations of rest houses and inns, length and walking time, altitude, steep sections of trail, tunnels which you must pass through and how you can get to and from the trail—by automobile or bus, walks where it is necessary to wear sturdy boots, carry your own food and drink, hire a guide or take along a flashlight are also indicated by symbols. A foldout map in the front of the book shows all the walks described. Just looking at the photographs will make you want to walk in Madeira. Available for a nominal charge from the tourist office in Funchal.

The following book provides an excellent introduction to Madeira. It contains just about all the information you need for planning and enjoying a holiday in Madeira, including a section describing walks:

• Madeira: Somewhere Special (in English) by Frank Cook. Gives information on accommodation, restaurants, nightlife, island history and culture, recreational activities, sightseeing, shopping, local transportation and travel arrangements. A section on walking includes a chart listing 20 walks, a map showing the routes and an introduction discussing weather, proper clothing and the system used for grading walks. The chart indicates the distance and required time for each path, its difficulty, the starting point, whether the walk has any steep sections and other information. Available from local bookstores or the Direcção Regional de Turismo.

Trailside Lodgings

Although no walk in the Madeiran mountains takes longer than a day to complete, several paths can be linked up to form longer excursions. A few mountain huts and inns provide accommodation in the central mountains. Elsewhere, it will be necessary to camp out, but you must be sure to check with the tourist office on where you can and cannot camp before you set out.

Mountain huts are located at Pico Ruivo, Estanquinhos and Bica da Cana, all above 1,500 meters (4,900 feet) elevation. Mountain inns are situated at Queimadas, Vinháticos and Rabaçal. For more information, contact the Direcção Regional de Turismo (see Address Directory), which owns the inn at Vinháticos and the Pico Ruivo hut.

Refuge locations are shown on maps contained in the guidebooks described above.

Madeira also has a wide variety of hotels, apartment hotels, inns and guesthouses. A booklet entitled Hotels describes available lodgings and can be obtained from the Direcção Regional de Turismo.

Camping

You can camp in some uncultivated areas in Madeira, but not without first asking if you may do so. Before camping on private property, you must ask the landowner's permission. If you don't, trespassing and vagrancy laws apply. Because it is not always obvious what is and is not private property or whom you should ask for permission, it is best to check your proposed campsites with the tourist office in Funchal in advance of your walk. They can tell you where you can and cannot camp.

Equipment Notes

When walking in the mountains you should take along a sweater or wind jacket in the summer; temperatures can be cool even on days when coastal areas are sweltering. At the same time, however, the sun can be intense, so a protective hat is recommended. During the winter, you should carry raingear in addition to warm clothing.

Comfortable walking shoes are adequate for the gentle trails that follow the levadas. Elsewhere, sturdy lug-soled hiking boots should be worn. The guidebooks described earlier indicate appropriate footwear for each trail. On some of the longer paths, you will want to take a lunch along.

It is also a good idea to carry map and compass on the more rugged mountain routes.

Guide Services

The tourist office recommends that walkers hire local guides to accompany them on a few of the more difficult mountain trails. Experienced mountaineers may find this unnecessary, but if you do wish to retain a guide, contact the Direcção Regional de Turismo.

Transportation

Buses run from Funchal to all parts of Madeira. You can take a bus to the starting points of most footpaths and catch one for a return trip at the end of your walk. A booklet containing bus service time tables and fare schedules, as well as information on car rental, is available from the Direcção Regional de Turismo. Also see *Madeira: Somewhere Special* in the section on *Guidebooks*.

How to Get There

Regularly scheduled flights link Madeira with Africa, the Americas, Portugal and the rest of Western Europe. Numerous cruise ships also visit the islands. For more information, contact your travel agent.

Useful Addresses & Telephone Numbers

General Tourist Information

In Madeira:

Direcção Regional de Turismo (see *Address Directory*).

In Portugal:

Direcção-Geral do Turismo (see *Address Directory*).

Abroad:

Information on Madeira can be obtained from the Portuguese National Tourist Offices in EUROPE: Amsterdam, Barcelona, Brussels, Copenhagen, Frankfurt, Geneva, London, Madrid, Milan, Paris, Stockholm, Vienna and Vigo; CANADA: Montreal and Toronto; and the U.S.A.: Chicago, Los Angeles and New York.

London: Portuguese National Tourist Office, New Bond House, 1/5 New Bond Street, London WIY ODB. Tel. (01) 493 3873.

New York: Portuguese National Tourist Office, 548 Fifth Avenue, New York, New York 10036. Tel. (212) 354-4403.

Search & Rescue

In case of accident or emergency, call the:

Fire Brigade: Tel. 2 91 15.

Suggested Walks

From Paúl da Serra to Ribeira da Janela. Over the rolling moorland of Paúl da Serra and down the densely wooded ridge east of the Janela River to a village on the northwest coast. Views of mountains and the sea. **Length:** 18 kilometers. **Walking Time:** 7 hours. **Difficulty:** Moderately difficult, with many ups and downs. **Path Markings:** Yellow circles containing directional arrows.
Map:
• Instituto Geográfico e Cadastral 1:50,000, sheet *Ilha da Madeira* (W).

From Pico do Arieiro to Encumeada. Madeira's grand mountain tour, including a possible walk to the top of Pico Ruivo, highest peak on the island. Route passes through a 100-meter tunnel in which a flashlight is required. Spectacular views of rugged crags and pinnacles and of deep, densely forested mountain gorges. **Length:** 21 kilometers. **Walking Time:** 8 hours. **Difficulty:** Difficult. **Path Markings:** Yellow circles containing directional arrows.
Special Note: Only experienced mountain travelers familiar with the use of map and compass should attempt this route alone. Others should hire a local guide to accompany them (see the section on *Guide Services*).
Maps:
• Instituto Geográfico e Cadastral 1:50,000, sheets *Ilha da Madeira (W)* and *Ilha da Madeira (E)*.

From Ribeiro Frio to Choupana. Lovely gentle mountain walk with spectacular views of rugged peaks and forested valleys. Much of the route follows levadas (irrigation canals). **Length:** 25 kilometers. **Walking Time:** 8-1/2 hours. **Difficulty:** Easy. **Path Markings:** Yellow circles containing directional arrows.
Map:
• Instituto Geográfico e Cadastral 1:50,000, sheet *Ilha da Madeira (E)*.

Address Directory

D

• *Direcção-Geral do Turismo,* Avenida António Augusto de Aguiar 86, Apartado 1929. P-1099 Lisboa, Portugal. Tel. Lisbon 57 55 27.
• *Direcção Regional de Turismo,* Avenida Arriaga 18, Funchal/ Madeira. Tel. 2 90 57.

E

- *Emergency:* Fire Brigade: Tel. 2 91 15.

I

- *Instituto Geográfico e Cadastral,* Venda de Cartas, Praça da Estrela, P-1200 Lisboa, Portugal.

P

- *Portuguese National Tourist Office, London,* New Bond House, 1/5 New Bond Street, London W1Y ODB. Tel. (01) 493 3873.
- *Portuguese National Tourist Office, New York,* 548 Fifth Avenue, New York, New York 10036. Tel. (212) 354-4403.

A Quick Reference

In a hurry? Turn to the following pages. They will give you the most important information on walking in Madeira.

Search & Rescue, page 50.

Weather Forecasts, page 46.

Associations to Contact for Information:
    On Walking, page 47.
    Tourist Information, page 50.

Maps, page 47.

Equipment, page 49.

Address Directory, page 51.

Mallorca

MALLORCA, THE LARGEST OF SPAIN'S Balearic Islands—3,640 square kilometers, or 1,405 square miles—lies in the western Mediterranean east of Valencia and south of Barcelona. Along with the islands of Formentera, Ibiza and Menorca, it comprises one of Spain's 50 provinces. Ibiza, the closest island to Spain, is less than 100 kilometers from the mainland.

Mallorca's balmy climate and spectacular white-sand beaches have made it a popular tourist area with both Europeans and Americans. But for those who prefer to escape the resort atmosphere, if only for a day, there are footpaths leading to quiet, sunny valleys and to high ridges with spectacular views of the island and the sea.

Mountains parallel Mallorca's northwest and southeast coasts. Between them lies a broad central lowland whose fertile soils support vast groves of olives, figs, apricots, oranges, lemons and almonds. The western mountains culminate in 1,443-meter (4,740-foot) Puig Major, the highest peak in the Baleares. Precipitous cliffs more than 305 meters (1,000 feet) high occur along the northwest coast where the mountains drop into the sea.

The eastern mountains comprise an eroded plateau with an average elevation of 300 meters. Beneath the hills are numerous limestone caves and subterranean lakes.

Mallorca is heavily wooded with extensive woodlands of pine and oak. Olive trees more than a thousand years old, gnarled and twisted by the centuries, grow on rocky slopes in the mountains and along the coast. There are also numerous rocky gorges, sandy rock-bound inlets and winding back roads that lead through sun-washed orchards, all of which can be explored on foot.

Climate

Mallorca has a typically Mediterranean climate with warm, dry summers and mild winters. The average minimum temperature in February, the coldest month of the year, is only 4°C. (39°F.). The average maximum temperature in July, the hottest month, is 32.8° C. (91°F.). The island has an average of 286 sunny days a year, including 146 in the months from October through April—the so-called "rainy season." Measurable pre-

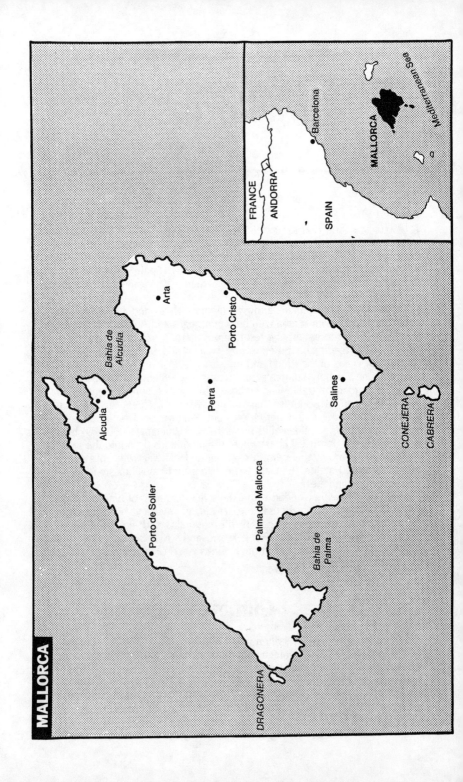

cipitation falls on an average of 66 days a year, almost all of which occurs in this period. Snow is virtually unknown even at higher elevations. Prevailing winds are southwesterly, and refreshing ocean breezes moderate the climate almost year round, the exception being a few still, hot weeks in midsummer. You can walk in Mallorca every month of the year, but the best times are spring and autumn when temperatures are mild.

Weather Forecasts

There is no telephone number you can call in Mallorca to obtain recorded weather forecasts. Generally, Mallorca's weather is such that a weather forecast is unnecessary, providing you carry a warm shirt or sweater and lightweight wind jacket for walks in the mountains should the weather change unexpectedly. General forecasts are broadcast on radio and television stations and appear in newspapers. You can also call the tourist office—Tel. 21 22 16—to get a rough idea of anticipated weather conditions.

Where to Get Walking Information

The best source of walking information in Mallorca is:

Federación Española de Montañismo (for its address, see the *Address Directory* at the back of this chapter). Affiliated with 12 local clubs devoted to mountaineering and cave exploration. The volunteer club members will answer specific questions on walking in Mallorca. (For hints on writing walking clubs, see the chapter on *Trail Information— and Where to Get It* in Part I.) Correspondence should be in Spanish or Catalan only.

You can also obtain information from:

See *Address Directory*:

Grupo Excursionista Mallorca. Correspondence in Spanish or Catalan only.

Sección Muntanya Club Pollença. Correspondence in Spanish or Catalan only.

Although Mallorca offers the best walking opportunities in the Balearic Islands, walks are also possible on the neighboring island of Menorca. For information you may contact:

Grupo Excursionista Joan Mercadal, or:
Sección Montaña Colegio la Salle (see *Address Directory*).

Few walking possibilities exist on the islands of Ibiza and Formentera.

Maps

The Balearic Islands are covered by 26 topographical sheets in a scale of 1:50,000. The maps are published by:

> **Instituto Geográfico y Catastral** (see *Address Directory*). Staff understands Spanish and French.

A free index, price list and maps can be obtained from the I.G.C. by mail. When ordering, you should specify the name and sheet number of each map you need.
You can also obtain the maps in Mallorca from:

> **Capitania General** (see *Address Directory*).

In addition, a general map of Mallorca in a scale of 1:31,250 is available from:

> **Libreria Lance** (see *Address Directory*).

Guidebooks

Three walking guides are available for Mallorca:

- *50 Excursiones a Pie por la Isla de Mallorca* (in Spanish) by Gabriel Font Martorell. Available from Fomento de Turismo (see *Address Directory*).
- *Guia de Excursiones por el Termino de Pollença* (in Spanish) by Seccion Montaña Club Pollença.
- *Rutes Amagados de Mallorca* (in Spanish) by Jesus Garcia Pastor. Describes 120 walks. Available from the author. (Recommended)

The guidebooks can also be obtained in most of the principal sport shops in Palma de Mallorca, such as Kenia, Tot Sport and Es Refugi (see *Address Directory*).

Trailside Lodgings

There are a few trailside refuges in Mallorca, none of which are in good condition. Accommodation in these huts is therefore somewhat primitive. If you plan to use the huts, be sure to take your own bedding and cooking equipment. The two principal refuges are *Es Cornador*, located on the mountain of the same name 10 kilometers from the village of Sóller, and *Sa Gubia*, also located on Monte Es Cornador, 10 kilometers from the village of Buñola.

Most walks on Mallorca, however, can be completed in a single day, so trailside lodgings are really not necessary. For a list of lodgings in towns and villages, you should write the Oficina de Información de Turismo in Palma de Mallorca (see *Address Directory*).

Camping

If you prefer to camp, you may do so in some areas of the mountains, although open camping is generally discouraged. There is usually little need for a tent—except when you don't have one. Just in case it does rain, it is advisable to carry a tarp during the summer and early autumn. And for the "rainy season" from October to April, you might want to consider a light tent. But you will have to choose the spot where you pitch camp carefully. There are quite a few restrictions on open camping. You cannot, for instance, light a fire. Nor can you camp within one kilometer of a town or village, within 50 meters of a road, on the beach, within 150 meters of a water supply, near historical sites or buildings, in forestry areas without the permission of the *Servicio Forestal*, nor on private land without the permission of the property owner. Best to check first with the tourist office to find out where you *can* camp.

Water

Tap water throughout Mallorca is safe to drink unless posted with a sign which says *agua non potable*. You should rely on this for your water needs, and carry a water bottle with you. Streams are few and far between and are sometimes filled only with rocks.

Equipment Notes

In summer, light loose-fitting clothing is the most comfortable wear. Many people hike—and, in fact, almost live—in shorts, which makes a lot of sense. A wide-brim hat is advisable, as is a supply of salt tablets. A lightweight wind jacket should be standard equipment no matter where you walk, and Mallorca is no exception. Long pants or knee breeches, a wind jacket, raingear and a sweater may be necessary at higher elevations in the winter. If you plan to use the trailside huts or camp out, be sure to take bedding and cooking equipment, as well as food and personal items.

Transportation

Railway and bus lines connect Palma with most other towns on Mallorca. A list of routes for both is found in the booklet, *Mallorca: General Information* (description below). For more information, contact the Oficina de Información de Turismo.

How to Get There

Mallorca is serviced by daily flights from Europe and North Africa. Ship crossings occur daily between Palma and the Spanish mainland. For more information, consult the booklet *Mallorca: General Information* (description below) or your travel agent.

Useful Addresses & Telephone Numbers

General Tourist Information

In Mallorca:

Oficina de Información de Turismo (see *Address Directory*). Staff speaks Catalan, Spanish, French, German and English. Useful publications include:

* *Mallorca: General Information* (in English; also available in other languages). Gives brief information on points of interest, climate,

accommodation, religious services, cuisine, transportation, cultural facilities, shopping, recreational activities and organized excursions. Includes a list of useful addresses and a street map of Palma de Mallorca.

Abroad:

Information on Mallorca can be obtained from branch offices of the Spanish National Tourist Office in EUROPE: Brussels, Copenhagen, Düsseldorf, Frankfurt, Geneva, Hamburg, Helsinki, The Hague, Lisbon, London, Milan, Munich, Oslo, Paris, Rome, Stockholm, Vienna and Zurich; JAPAN: Tokyo; CANADA: Toronto; and the U.S.A.: Chicago, San Francisco and New York.

London: Spanish National Tourist Office, 57-58 St. James Street, London SW1A 1LD. Tel. (01) 499 1095.

New York: Spanish National Tourist Office, 665 Fifth Avenue, New York, New York 10022. Tel. (212) 759-8822.

Sport Shops

The selection of walking and mountaineering equipment in the sport shops in Mallorca generally takes a backseat to tennis racquets, scuba diving gear, rubber rafts and beach wear. Nonetheless, some hiking and climbing gear—and the guidebooks to walking on the island—can be found at the following shops, all located in Palma de Mallorca (see *Address Directory*):

Kenia
Tot Sport
Es Refugi
Deportes Rado

Search & Rescue

In an emergency: Find the nearest telephone and call the police. Tel. 21 12 21.

Suggested Walk

From Pollença to Galilea. Through the mountains of northwestern Mallorca: pine forests, rocky peaks, spectacular views. **Walking Time:** 4

days. **Difficulty:** Moderately difficult to difficult (several steep ascents).
Path Markings: Unmarked.
Maps:
* I.G.C. Mapa Nacional Topografico 1:50,000, sheets 644 Pollença, 670 *Soller*, 671 *Inca* and 698 *Palma*.

Address Directory

C

* *Capitania General*, Piaza Almudaina, n 1, Palma de Mallorca.

D

* *Deportes Rado*, Calle de Arzobispo Aspargo 25, Palma de Mallorca.

E

* *Emergency:* Tel. 21 12 21.
* *Es Refugi*, Oms 15, Palma de Mallorca.

F

* *Federación Española de Montañismo*, Delegación en Baleares, Pedro Alcántara Peña 13, Palma de Mallorca. No telephone.
* *Fomento de Turismo*, Paseo del Borne, Palma de Mallorca.

G

* *Grupo Excursionista Joan Mercadal*, Norte 10, Mahon, Menorca. Tel. 35 14 00.
* *Grupo Excursionista Mallorca*, Estudio General 17, Palma de Mallorca. No telephone.

I

* *Instituto Geográfico y Catastral*, Calle General Ibáñez de Ibero 3, Madrid 3, Spain. Tel. (91) 234 5116.

J

* *Jesus Garcia Pastor*, see Pastor, Jesus Garcia.

K

- *Kenia*, Calle de Call 1, Palma de Mallorca.

L

- *Libreria Lance*, Calle Huetos, Palma de Mallorca.

O

- *Oficina de Información de Turismo*, Avenida Rey Jaime III, 10, Palma de Mallorca. Tel. (971) 21 22 16.

P

- *Pastor, Jesus Garcia*, Calle de Ramon Llull, Palma de Mallorca.

S

- *Sección Montana Colegio la Salle*, cta. San Clemente s/n, Menorca.
- *Sección Muntanya Club Pollença*, La Plaza 1, Pollensa, Mallorca. Tel. (971) 53 00 00.
- *Spanish National Tourist Office, London*, 57-58 St. James Street, London SW1A 1LD. Tel. (01) 499 1095.
- *Spanish National Tourist Office, New York*, 665 Fifth Avenue, New York, New York 10022. Tel. (212) 759-8822.

T

- *Tot Sport*, Plaza Weyler, Palma de Mallorca.

A Quick Reference

In a hurry? Turn to the pages listed below. They will give you the most important information on walking in Mallorca.

Search & Rescue, page 59.

Weather Forecasts, page 55.

Associations to Contact for Information:
On Walking, page 55.
Tourist Information, page 58.

Maps, page 56.

Equipment, page 58.

Address Directory, page 60.

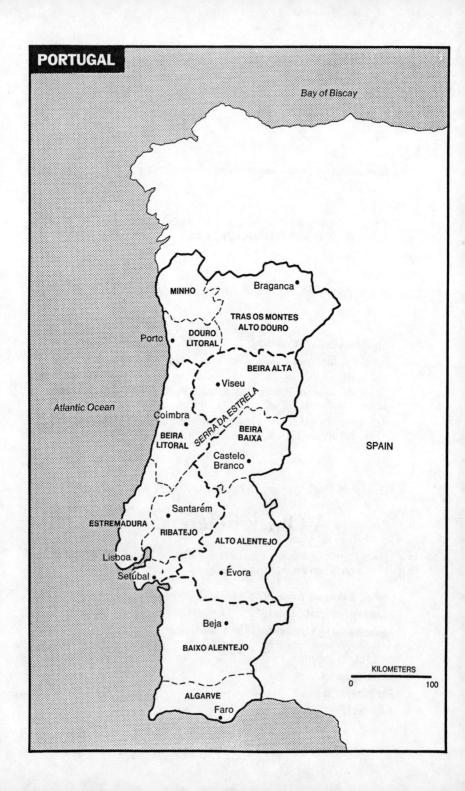

Portugal

PORTUGAL IS NOT A COUNTRY one would normally visit specifically to go hiking. There are no marked footpaths, trailside refuges, walking clubs or other organizations able to provide information on the trails or the possibilities for rambles. The only guidebook for walkers describes the paths on the island of Madeira, which lies in the Atlantic off the coast of Africa. The main tourist office, in fact, might even claim that hiking does not exist in the country. Several tourist brochures published by local tourist offices in northern Portugal list "mountain walks" as one of the attractions of their areas. But no other details are given. And attempting to obtain further information from the tourist offices is fruitless.

The Portuguese themselves walk a great deal as it happens—but out of necessity. And therein lies their indifference to walking for pleasure. They'd give anything to ride for a change. That's their idea of sport and pleasure—not walking.

As a result, they are likely to view a person who voluntarily shoulders a pack and walks through the countryside as something of an oddity. And local residents have no compunction about staring at a foreign walker, especially if the import is decked out in climbing breeches and kneesocks. But after they recover from their initial shock, the people are disarmingly friendly. A nod of greeting and a *"bom dia"* will bring a smile—and sometimes an invitation to share a glass of wine or a simple meal.

Portugal is, in fact, a beautiful country in which to walk, and numerous routes are possible. It is covered by a dense network of footpaths and rural tracks, routes of local commerce and communication that have been in use for centuries. As a result, you can walk almost anywhere in Portugal—along the rocky Algarve coast; through the woodlands and rolling hills of the Alentejo; up the steep, forested ridges of the northern mountains to open summits with panoramic views; and in fertile river valleys where terraced vineyards climb the slopes on either side.

Walkers in Portugal, however, are very much on their own. Those used to explicit guidebooks, special walking maps, well marked footpaths and comfortable trailside refuges may find the situation inconvenient at best, somewhat intimidating at worst. Yet it would be a mistake to ignore walking possibilities in Portugal simply because the Portuguese have not bothered to spell them out. The inconvenience occasioned by the lack of walking information is more than made up for by the sheer adventure of discovery and the refreshing absence of the hordes of summertime walkers so often encountered elsewhere in Europe.

To go walking in Portugal, you must buy the 1:50,000 topographical maps published by the *Instituto Geográfico e Cadastral* and plan your own routes. These maps cover the entire country and show all footpaths and rural tracks. A quick glance at virtually any sheet will suggest countless possibilities. All you have to do is decide where you want to walk (see the regional descriptions later in this chapter), plot out your route on the appropriate maps and start walking.

Portugal covers 89,060 square kilometers (34,386 square miles)— roughly 15 percent of the Iberian Peninsula, which it shares with Spain. From north to south, the longest distance is 561 kilometers (348 miles); from east to west, 218 kilometers (135 miles). Cabo Roca, a rocky headland west of Lisbon, is the westernmost point in continental Europe.

The capital city of Lisbon is situated on a large estuary at the mouth of the Rio Tejo, which rises in Spain and flows westward across the center of Portugal, dividing the country into two more or less distinct geographical regions. The country north of the Tejo largely consists of plateaus cut by deep river valleys and surmounted by numerous mountain ranges. The highest range is the Serra da Estrela, which culminates in 1,993-meter (6,539-foot) Torre peak. Roughly 90 percent of the land north of the Rio Tejo exceeds 396 meters (1,300 feet).

The terrain south of the Tejo consists of gently undulating plains and broad river basins, with occasional outcrops of hills. Only one range, the Serra de São Mamede, along the Spanish border, exceeds 1,000 meters (3,280 feet). The plains of Alentejo, which cover much of southern Portugal, range in elevation from about 490 meters (1,600 feet) in the north to 215 meters (700 feet) in the south.

The great majority of Portugal's 9 million residents live in the countryside. Lisbon has just under a million people; Porto just over 300,000. No other towns in the country exceed 50,000 population. The most densely populated region is the northern half of the country, particularly the coastal provinces. Rural poverty is widespread in this region because the land is not productive enough to support so many people. Yet the Portuguese endure their lot with surprising good humor and stoic grace. Even the poorest are proudly willing to share whatever they have.

Portugal is one of the oldest nations in Europe, having become a united kingdom in 1153. Its current frontiers were established in 1297, although Portugal also considers such farflung domains as the Azores, Madeira and Macau, an island in the South China Sea, as integral parts of the country. Portuguese is the native tongue of some 140 million people, most of whom live in Brazil. The language bears a superficial resemblance to Spanish, but is actually a distinct tongue that differs in numerous important ways. Few Portuguese living outside of Lisbon, Porto or major resort areas speak a second language. Visitors who speak Spanish, or even Italian, may be able to communicate, albeit imperfectly, but those who do not should carry a Portuguese dictionary or phrasebook.

Hemmed in by Spain on the east, facing the Atlantic horizon on the west, Portugal has always been a seafaring nation. And it is no wonder that this tiny kingdom on the western extremity of Europe played the instrumental role in opening the great Age of Discovery in the 15th and 16th centuries. Dom Henrique o Navegador—Prince Henry the Navigator—(1394-1460) reformulated, after centuries of disuse, the science of navigation, which he taught to the Portuguese captains who set off in their tiny caravels to explore the coast of Africa and beyond. The school of seamanship and navigation he founded at Sagres, on Portugal's southern coast, lived after him, and here such explorers as Vasco da Gama and Christopher Columbus learned the arts of seamanship and of reckoning by the stars.

Portugal, for a time, was one of the richest and most powerful nations in the world. Today, like other colonial powers, its golden age is past, but the intimate relationship with the sea remains. Portuguese fishermen still ply the Atlantic, searching now for wealth of a different kind. Boats, nets, the smell of seaweed and fish—these are familiar elements in the lives of numerous small villages facing the sea, from the rocky bluffs of Algarve to the wooded dunes of Minho. And in many of the coastal villages, such as Nazaré, the fishermen still wear their traditional long black stocking caps and push their gaily-painted, high-prowed boats into the surf at dawn each morning with a heave of their shoulders.

Flora & Fauna

Some 2,500 species of herbs, shrubs and trees are found in Portugal. Deciduous Atlantic species predominate in the cooler, more humid north, evergreen Mediterranean and North African types in the south. About two-thirds of the flora consist of plants generally distributed throughout Western Europe. The rest are characteristic of the Iberian Peninsula and Africa. Endemics includes species of campion, rock cress, saxifrage, narcissus and asphodel. A rhododendron native to the Iberian Peninsula is protected in a botanical reserve at Cambarinho, in the Serra do Caramulo. Plans are now underway to identify and protect other rare and endangered species.

North of the Rio Tejo, the countryside is mostly wooded. Forests of maritime pine line much of the coast, where they were planted to stabilize dunes. Inland, woodlands dominated by English oak, Pyrenean oak and Portuguese oak are widespread. Chestnuts, lindens, elms, poplars, and olive trees are also common. Pine forests are again encountered in the mountains, but there maritime pine is replaced by other species. Altogether, woodland and forest cover about 20 percent of Portugal.

South of the Rio Tejo, the forests give way to broad, open grasslands and several evergreen scrub formations. Scattered woodlands, dominated by cork oak and holm oak, occur as islands in the predominantly treeless plains. Along the coast, Italian stone pine replaces the maritime pine of the north. Eucalyptuses, which are native to Australia, have been widely planted in the region. So have acacias, especially along the coast where they, like the pines, are used to stabilize dunes.

Most of the valleys and plains are intensively cultivated. The most important crops in the north are wine grapes, from which Port wine is made, as well as fine red and white table wines. Vineyards cover fertile valley floors winding through the mountains and spread up the nearby slopes on successions of terraces. Maize is also grown in the north and rice is cultivated in the marshier portions of some river valleys, including those of the Rio Mondego and Rio Tejo.

The rolling plains of the Alentejo are a sea of wheat fields. But the region is best known for its groves of cork oaks, whose spongy outer bark is used in the manufacture of commercial cork—of which Portugal is the world's chief supplier. (The next time you open a bottle of wine, look at the cork. Chances are it began its journey to your table from an Alentejo cork grove.) Olives and carob trees are also grown commercially in the Alentejo.

The Algarve region supplies olives, figs, almonds and other fruits. During January and February, the trees burst into blossom, turning entire hillsides into feathery white mounds above the azure waters of the coastal inlets.

Portugal is one of the last remaining countries in Western Europe to have a native wolf population. Wolves occur in the northern mountains and along the Spanish border. A few wild boars also frequent the same regions. Other mammals include the rabbit, squirrel, fox, roe deer and elk. A few lynx, which are strictly protected, occur in wilder areas, and a small seal population frequents the coast. Birds are those typical of the Iberian Peninsula, but also include numerous migrants, winter visitors and occasional stragglers from North Africa.

The only poisonous snake is the viper, which is fairly common in some areas. The best protection against being bitten is to watch carefully where you place your hands and feet and to wear boots that cover the ankles. You are unlikely to encounter a viper in any case, but in the event of a bite seek medical attention at once.

Mosquitoes can be a nuisance during May and June in some areas, particularly near Coimbra and Figueira da Foz. Although malaria was once a problem in Portugal, it was eliminated about 40 years ago. Today, there is no cause for worry. During May and June, however, it is advisable to carry insect repellent simply for the sake of comfort.

Climate

Although Portugal faces the Atlantic, its climate is Mediterranean, with warm, dry summers and mild, wet winters. The northern half of the country, which is partly affected by climatic events occurring even farther north, tends to be somewhat cooler and moister year round than the south, but still shares the same basic climatic pattern.

Portugal's climate is moderated by the Atlantic Ocean, in particular by the Gulf Stream. Move away from the coast, and temperatures become higher in summer and lower in winter. For example, the mean low temperature during the winter in the town of Viana do Castelo, on Portugal's northern coast, is 5.1°C. (41°F.). Yet the town of Bragança, 160 kilometers due east, experiences an average minimum temperature in January of 0°C. (32°F.).

Similarly, ocean breezes during the summer keep coastal areas cooler than the interior. For instance, the mean high temperature during the summer reaches 39°C. (102°F.) at Beja, a town in the southern interior of Baixo Alentejo, while the town of Faro, situated on the Algarve coast more than 100 kilometers due south, has a mean high temperature in July of only 28.2°C. (82.8°F.).

Algarve, the southernmost province, is also the driest, receiving an average of 420 mm (16.5 inches) of rain per year. Nearly 98 percent of this rain falls during the months from November through February. Yet even during the so-called rainy season, the sun shines on the Algarve more than 60 percent of the time. Daytime highs during the winter average a balmy 19°C. (66°F.); nighttime lows, a mere 8°C. (46°F.).

Northern Portugal, particularly along the coast, receives many times more rainfall than the south. Viana do Castelo, for instance, receives an average annual rainfall of 1,562 mm (61.5 inches). And while 92 percent of this falls during the September-to-May period, the summer months bring an average of 126 mm (5 inches)—15 times the amount experienced in the Algarve during the same season.

Northern Portugal also experiences wide differences in temperature and rainfall over relatively short distances—the result of its numerous mountain ranges, which greatly affect the flow of air and moisture. One locality may receive as little as 500 mm (19.7 inches) of precipitation per year, and have average temperatures that range from a high in July of 31.8°C. (89°F.) to a low in January of 1.8°C. (35°F.), while another locality, only 50 kilometers away, may receive three times as much precipitation and have average temperatures that are as much as 7°C. (13°F.) cooler in July and 2°C. (3.6°F.) warmer in January.

As with any mountainous region, however, the mountains themselves are both cooler and wetter throughout the year than the surrounding lowlands. The village of Penhas Douradas, for instance, situated in the Serra da Estrela at an elevation of 1,549 meters (5,082 feet), receives an average of 1,916 mm (75 inches) of precipitation per year, much of it in the form of snow, and experiences average temperatures ranging from a high in July of 21.7°C. (71°F.) to a low in January of *minus* 0.4°C. (31.3°F.).

Consequently, if you plan to walk in the mountains of northern Portugal, you should be sure to always carry spare warm clothing, windproof outer clothing and raingear—even in the summer.

Weather Forecasts

You can obtain weather forecasts by telephoning the National Meteorological and Geophysical Institute in Lisbon:

> **Instituto Nacional de Meteorologia e Geofisica.** Tel. 80 21 19. Staff speaks only Portuguese. Calls are accepted only after 2 p.m.

When obtaining a forecast, be sure to specify the particular region and weather information that interests you—temperature, precipitation, wind and so on.

Where to Get Walking Information

Information on walking is simply unavailable in Portugal. There are no walking clubs, guidebooks, marked paths, trailside refuges or any of the other amenities to which walkers have grown accustomed in other European countries.

To plan walks in Portugal, first get as much information as you can about the various regions. The regional descriptions in this chapter will get you started. They describe the outstanding features of each region, list appropriate maps, suggest several walking possibilities and provide the names of the main tourist offices. From these offices you can obtain descriptive brochures that will further help you to decide where to walk. The general guidebooks mentioned below may also be helpful. Then, after deciding where you want to walk, obtain a lodging list (see below) and the appropriate 1:50,000 topographical maps and plot out your route.

Those who wish to climb in Portugal, say in the Serra da Estrela, may be able to obtain some assistance from Portugal's national mountaineering club:

> **Clube Nacional de Montanhismo** (for its address and telephone number, see the *Address Directory* at the back of this chapter).

The club, however, is small and is devoted primarily to the interests of its members. It cannot provide any information on walking in Portugal. Its voluntary secretary will occasionally answer specific questions on climbing, but you must write in Portuguese or Spanish.

Maps

Portugal is covered by 173 five-color topographical maps in a scale of 1:50,000. The maps show both country tracks and footpaths as well as features of vegetation and terrain. Some of the sheets have not been updated for several years, so you should be prepared for possible inconsistencies between what the maps show and what you find on the ground. On the whole, however, the maps are extremely accurate and a glance at almost any sheet will suggest numerous possible walks. If it were not for these maps, hiking in Portugal would be almost impossible. The maps constitute the only information on walking routes available in Portugal. They are published by:

Instituto Geográfico e Cadastral (see *Address Directory*). You may write in English, French, Spanish or Portuguese. The maps may be ordered by mail, and a catalog, *Cartas e Publicações*, with an index and sample maps, is available upon request.

The maps are available nowhere else in the country.

Guidebooks

There are no guidebooks to the footpaths in Portugal. There is, however, an excellent series of general guidebooks—the *Colecção Turismo*—covering 13 regions in the country. When used in conjunction with the 1:50,000 topographical maps, these guides will help you decide where to walk and what to see enroute. The text of each guide is printed in Portuguese, French, English and German. The guides in the series include:

- *Lisboa* by Ferreira de Andrade, Colecção Turismo No. 1
- *Castelos de Portugal* by Dr. Manuel Ivo Cruz, Colecção Turismo No.2
- *Porto* by Dr. Noël de Arriaga, Colecção Turismo No. 3
- *Coimbra* by Manuel Chaves e Castro, Colecção Turismo No. 4
- *Alcobaça, Batalha, Fátima, Nazaré, Leiria* by Dr. Noël de Arriaga, Colecção Turismo No. 5
- *Sintra* by Gonçalo de Santa Maria, Colecção Turismo No. 6
- *Estoril* by Francisco Mata, Colecção Turismo No. 8
- *Ribatejo* by Calderon Dinís, Colecção Turismo No. 10
- *Algarve* by Dr. Jorge Felner da Costa, Colecção Turismo No. 13
- *Braga e seu Distrito* by Calderon Dinís, Colecção Turismo No. 14

- *Viana do Castelo e seu Distrito* by Calderon Dinís, Colecção Turismo No. 15
- *Cascais* by Ferreira de Andrade, Colecção Turismo No. 16
- *Fátima* by Dr. Jorge Felner da Costa, Colecção Turismo No. 17.

The guides and a list of new titles can be obtained by mail from their publisher:

Editorial de Publicações Turísticas (see *Address Directory*).

The guides may also be purchased at many bookstores in the regions they cover.

Trailside Lodgings

Because Portugal has no trailside refuges, walkers who wish to avoid camping must plan their itineraries so that each day's walk leads to a town or village offering overnight accommodation. A wide variety of lodgings is available, including hotels, state-operated inns *(pousadas)*, privately owned inns *(estalagens)*, pensions *(pensões)* and youth hostels. Rates also vary widely, ranging from astronomical in some of the hotels at the coastal resorts to unbelievably inexpensive in the homey pensões in rural villages. The more than two dozen pousadas scattered throughout Portugal offer deluxe accommodation in remodeled castles, palaces, monasteries and other historical buildings situated in scenic locales. Room rates in the pousadas are not cheap—at least not by Portuguese standards—but they are surprisingly reasonable for what you get. The true travel bargains, however, are found in Portugal's youth hostels and pensões. With a little shopping, you can often find a bright, airy room for two with a bath in one of the pensões for about half as much as it would cost two people to eat a simple meal in a restaurant in Germany or Switzerland.

Full details on Portugal's hotels, motels, pousadas, private inns and pensions are given in a comprehensive lodging directory:

- *Portugal: Hoteis/Hotels* (in Portuguese, French, English and German). Lists all lodgings by town. Gives the address, telephone number and range of prices for each lodging. Indicates available facilities through symbols. Available from the Direcção-Geral do Turismo (see *Address Directory*).

A color brochure describing Portugal's pousadas is also available from the Direcção-Geral do Turismo.

Youth Hostels

Although the youth hostel movement is fairly new to Portugal, nearly a dozen hostels are already open and others are scheduled to open soon. There is no age limit, but you must have a valid international youth hostel card and a sheet sleeping bag to stay in the hostels. These can be purchased at some—but not all—hostels. Admission to the hostels is permitted anytime between 9 a.m. and 10 p.m. All of the hostels except those in São Bruno and Beja remain open all year. Reservations should be made directly to each hostel.

Further information on the hostels, including a list with their addresses and telephone numbers, is available from the Direcção-Geral do Turismo or the:

Associação Portuguesa de Pousadas de Juventude (see *Address Directory*).

Camping

Although camping in the open is not forbidden in Portugal, neither is it encouraged. As a rule, it is best to camp in established campgrounds *(parques de campismo)* wherever possible. Most campgrounds are open to everyone. To gain admittance, foreign campers must present their passports. Parks operated by the Federação Portuguesa de Campismo e Caravanismo, however, are open only to campers with valid camping carnets issued by the International Federation of Camping and Caravaning (FICC).

Full details on Portugal's campgrounds are given in the following guidebook:

* *Roteiro Campista: Guia de Parques de Campismo e de Turismo e das Casas Abrigo* (in Portuguese, French, English and German). Published annually by F. Pires da Silva and A. Almeida Henriques (see *Address Directory*). Lists more than 75 campgrounds, with maps showing local access routes. Gives addresses, telephone numbers, the names of proprietors and dates of operation. Symbols indicate the available facilities at each campground. Available from most bookstores and tourist offices.

A leaflet containing much of the same information, but lacking the local maps, is available free of charge from most tourist offices.

If you decide to camp away from established campgrounds, be sure to obey the regulations governing open camping in Portugal and to leave your site as undisturbed as it was before your arrival. The following regulations are designed to minimize the impact of campers on the

Portuguese landscape and should be strictly obeyed. Failure to do so could result in your being asked to move on by local authorities.

1. Camping is forbidden in urban areas; within 300 meters of campgrounds, beaches, and other public areas; and in zones set up to protect watersheds and public drinking-water facilities.
2. It is forbidden for groups larger than 20 people to camp in one location.
3. Campers must not foul spring or well water or light campfires within areas of brush or pines.
4. Campers are required to properly dispose of all refuse and ensure that upon departure the only evidence of their sites is no more than a few blades of flattened grass.

Water

When walking in Portugal, you should carry your own water. Natural water sources may be unsafe to drink, and it's difficult to know which ones are and which aren't. You can safely drink water from almost any tap, although fountains in small villages should usually be avoided.

Equipment Notes

During Portugal's warm, nearly rainless summers, loose-fitting shirts and walking shorts are perhaps the most comfortable clothing, although long pants and a wind jacket may be needed at times along the coast and at higher elevations. Sunglasses, a hat and a supply of salt tablets are also recommended when walking in Portugal's relentless summer sun.

Warmer clothing will often be necessary during the winter, despite its overall mildness. In addition, you should carry raingear from late September through April or May, the period during which Portugal receives most of its precipitation. In the north, raingear and a sweater may even be necessary on occasion during the summer months.

Although sturdy walking shoes are suitable for some rural tracks, many paths require lug-soled hiking boots, especially those in mountainous regions. Unless you are familiar with the terrain over which you intend to travel, it is best to wear boots from the start. That way, you'll be prepared for whatever comes.

Other essential items of gear include a full water bottle, the appropriate 1:50,000 topographical maps and a good compass. In the absence of trail descriptions and marked paths, skill in the use of map and compass is essential.

If you intend to camp out you will have to carry additional equipment as well as at least part of your food. Otherwise, you can travel lightly; in most parts of the country you will be within easy walking distance of towns and villages where food and accommodation are available.

Crowded Trails

Portugal has no crowded trails, which is one of the best reasons for walking in the country. For the walker who values solitude there are few places in Europe where it can be had so easily.

Walking Tours & Guides

There are neither walking tours nor guides in Portugal. It is strictly a country for those walkers who prefer to strike out on their own and for whom one of the greatest rewards is the thrill of discovering what lies around the next bend and over the following ridge.

Cross-Country Skiing

There are no cross-country ski centers or marked ski tracks in the mountains of Portugal. The Serra da Estrela in northern Portugal receive enough snow from January through March to support downhill skiing, especially near 1,993-meter (6,539-foot) Torre. Cross-country skiing is also possible in this area. But, again, you are very much on your own.

Trains & Buses

Eurail and Interrail passes are valid in Portugal. No other special fares or discount tickets are available. Regular train and bus fares, however, are fairly reasonable. Kilometer for kilometer buses are slightly cheaper than the trains. Their circuitous local routes also allow you to get to small, out-of-the-way villages which provide good starting points for walks in the countryside. For long trips you should rely on the trains.

Local bus schedules are posted in the stations. There is no single schedule that covers the entire country.

For information on rail service, you can contact:

Caminhos de Ferro Portugueses (see *Address Directory*).

Useful Addresses & Telephone Numbers

General Tourist Information

In Portugal:

Direcção-Geral do Turismo (see *Address Directory*). Staff speaks Portuguese, Spanish, French, German and English. Can provide a brochure listing the addresses and telephone numbers of local tourist offices throughout Portugal. Distributes numerous tourist information brochures, including:

* *Portugal Holiday Guide*
* *Portugal Welcomes You*
* *Your Companion in Portugal*

The Comissões Municipais de Turismo and Comissões Regionais de Turismo can provide numerous brochures describing their respective towns and regions. To obtain the addresses and telephone numbers of the municipal and regional tourist commissions, write to the Direcção-Geral do Turismo and ask for the following brochure:

* *Informação Turística No. 1: Orgãos Locais de Turismo.*

Abroad:

Branch offices of the Portuguese National Tourist Office are located in EUROPE: Amsterdam, Barcelona, Brussels, Copenhagen, Frankfurt, Geneva, London, Madrid, Milan, Paris, Stockholm, Vienna and Vigo; CANADA: Montreal and Toronto; and the U.S.A.: Chicago, Los Angeles and New York.

London: Portuguese National Tourist Office, New Bond Street House, 1st Floor Suite, 1/5 New Bond Street, London W1Y 0BD. Tel. (01) 49 338 73.

New York: Portuguese National Tourist Office, 548 Fifth Avenue, New York, New York 10036. Tel. (212) 354-4403.

Sport Shops

The following camping shops—all in Lisbon—have a limited selection of walking equipment:

See *Address Directory*:
Marcampo.
Solecampo.
Tecnicampo Lda.

There are also two shops which carry general sports equipment, including some camping and walking gear:

Casa Senna and
Casa Socidel (see *Address Directory*).

Search & Rescue

The police conduct search and rescue. In case of emergency, telephone:

Police Emergency: Tel. 115.

Long-Distance Footpaths

There are no long-distance footpaths in Portugal, although extended walks are possible by linking up existing footpaths and rural tracks.

Portugal's Walking Regions

Because unpaved rural tracks and footpaths are unmarked, it is not practicable to recommend specific routes. There are numerous possibilities, however, most of which are clearly evident on the 1:50,000 topographical maps covering Portugal. The following regional descriptions are intended to give you some idea of what to expect and to suggest certain areas within each region that are well worth exploring.

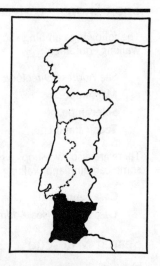

Algarve & Baixo Alentejo

For most foreign visitors, the broad, gently undulating plain of Baixo Alentejo is little more than a region one must get through to reach the spectacular Algarve coast. On the nine-hour train ride from Lisbon to Faro, the scene hardly ever seems to change: vast wheat fields stretch as far as the eye can see, occasionally broken by ravines and low hills covered with arid grassland and scrub. Oak woodlands are scattered in isolated islands across the plain, marking the pockets of ground moisture sufficient to support their growth. During the rainy season the plain is a vivid green, but by late spring it turns golden brown, and the summer heat beats down with a relentless ferocity out of a typically cloudless sky. From the train or a car a little bit of Baixo Alentejo goes a long way, and one soon begins to wish for the hills and scarps that mark its southern border with the Algarve.

The walker, however, sees a side of Baixo Alentejo that other travelers miss. No walker, of course, wants to walk through kilometer after kilometer of wheat fields with the prospect of only more wheat fields to follow. The rewards of walking quickly reach a diminishing return. But Baixo Alentejo can be enjoyed. To do so, you must scale it down—look for the small, the inscrutable, the subtle. Each ravine teems with life—the buzzing of insects, the frozen motion of a lizard peering at you from a rock, the rustle of a startled rabbit scampering for safety through the grass. Each hill top brings a view, perhaps of wheat fields, of small villages in the distance or of a tree-lined stream, alongside which a donkey plods head down in front of a cart on a dirt track. Isolated villages rarely visited by foreign tourists are scattered across the plain—villages that have changed little over the last century. To the west, large reservoirs nestle in shallow vales, and marshes and lagoons line the low-lying coast north of Cabo de Sines, providing a breeding ground for a rich variety of bird life. Near

Santiago do Cacém there are several Roman ruins and a splendid medieval castle. Another notable castle is the Alcácer Castle at Alcácer do Sal. And Beja, the provincial capital, is an ancient Roman town, founded in 48 B.C. by Julius Caesar. Baixo Alentejo is not a place for long walks. But short walks, say from Santiago do Cacém into the Serra de Grândola, from Moura into the Serra da Adiça above the southward-flowing Rio Guadiana, or from Santa Clara-a-Velha into the hills surrounding the Barragem de Santa Clara reservoir, do have their reward—not in the spectacular, but in the subtle, and in the contacts with the people who, for generations, have made their lives there.

To the south, the plain of Baixo Alentejo rises to meet the hills of the Algarve. Set off from the rest of the country and facing Africa to the south, the Algarve is the driest, sunniest region in Portugal. Along its coast are small, white-washed villages nestling in the folds of hills overlooking the sea; rocky sea bluffs fringed with prickly pear cactus, the tall stalks of the agave plant and cascades of flowers ringing sandy coves; and clusters of jagged sea stacks broken away from the mainland by the force of the waves. Multiple-story hotels, their straight boxy lines contrasting sharply with the typically Moorish architecture of the older buildings, now line the beaches of many of the once-peaceful fishing villages. Yet the old lifestyle still maintains a foothold. In several villages, the highest structure is still the church spire and old women dressed in black carry water from the town well on their donkeys. Gaily painted fishing boats bob at anchor in the coves as old fishermen sit at dockside mending their nets. And from village restaurants the smells of the day's catch being cooked wafts through the air—the ubiquitous grilled sardines; *caldeirada,* a chowder of different varieties of fish and shellfish combined with potatoes and tomatoes, richly laced with onions and garlic; *cataplana,* a combination of clams, ham and sausage flavored with onions and paprika; and *squid,* often cooked in its own ink.

Near the hotels during the summer, the beach is cluttered with golden bodies from all corners of Europe. But walk up the coast a bit, around one of the rocky headlands or through one of the sea arches carved in the coastal cliffs, and you can often find an uncrowded cove hemmed in by cliffs where azure waters lap against golden sand.

The Algarve coast is more or less divided by the town of Faro. To the east are long golden strands and sand dunes; to the west, a succession of cliffs, sandy coves and sea stacks, culminating in the eroded headlands of Cabo de São Vicente, the southwesternmost tip of Portugal. Below the cliffs of Cabo de São Vicente is the bay of Belixe, noted for its underwater caverns and rock formations, and nearby, the fishing village of Sagres where Prince Henry the Navigator established his school of seamanship in the 15th century, thus launching the Portuguese voyages of Magellan and Vasco da Gama.

Behind the coast, rolling hills slope gently northward, rising in the west to Serra do Espinhaco de Cão and the complex igneous massif of the Serra de Monchique, which attains an elevation of 902 meters (2,959 feet) before it drops sharply to the plain of Baixo Alentejo. To the east are the extensive Serra do Caldeirão and other, smaller hills cradling isolated streams. In the hills above Silves the hot springs of Caldas de Monchique are thought to have been a Roman spa where bathers sought relief from rheumatic pains. And here and there, in the principal valleys, are small villages surrounded by groves of olive, fig and almond trees.

Tourist Information

See *Address Directory*:

Comissão Municipal de Turismo de Beja.

Comissão Regional de Turismo do Algarve.

Tourist offices are also located in at least 10 other towns in the Algarve, including Albufeira, Portimão and Silves.

Maps

Algarve—Western (including the Serra de Monchique & Serra do Espinhaço de Cão): I.G.C. Carta Corográfica 1:50,000, sheets 48 D; 49 A, B, C and D; 51 B; and 52 A and B.

Algarve—Eastern: I.G.C. Carta Corográfica 1:50,000, sheets 50 A, B, C and D; and 53 A and B.

Algarve—Serra do Caldeirão: I.G.C. Carta Corográfica 1:50,000, sheets 49 B and D; and 50 A and C.

Baixo Alentejo—Northwestern (including Santiago do Cacém & the Serra de Grândola): I.G.C. Carta Corográfica 1:50,000, sheets 39 A, B, C and D; 42 A, B, C and D.

Baixo Alentejo—Northeastern (including Beja & the Serra da Adiça): I.G.C. Carta Corográfica 1:50,000, sheets 40 C; 43 A, B, C and D; and 44 A, B, C and D.

Baixo Alentejo—Southwestern (including Santa Cruz-a-Velha): I.G.C. Carta Corográfica 1:50,000, sheets 45 A, B, C and D; and 49 A and B.

Baixo Alentejo—Southeastern: I.G.C. Carta Corográfica 1:50,000, sheets 46 A, B, C and D; 47 A; and 50 A.

Suggested Walking Areas

The two best places to walk in southern Portugal are the Serra de Monchique, where numerous footpaths wander through the forest, along streams and to summits with splendid views, and along the rocky Algarve coast west of Faro. Other places to walk include the Serra do Espinhaço de Cão and Serra do Caldeirão in the Algarve, and the Serra de Grândola and the hills near Santa Clara-a-Velha in Baixo Alentejo.

Beira Alta, Beira Baixa & Alto Alentejo

These three provinces in east-central Portugal are bounded in the west and north by mountains and on the east by the Spanish frontier. To the south lies Baixo Alentejo.

The heart of Beira Alta, the northernmost of the three provinces, is an uplifted plain into which the Rio Mondego and Rio Vouga have cut deep valleys (known as *terra quente*—hot country). The plain, a westward extension of Spain's Meseta Plateau, is ringed to the north and west by a crescent of low mountain chains. Chief among these are the Serra de Montemuro, which rise to an elevation of 1,382 meters (4,534 feet) in the northwestern corner of Beira Alta; and the Serra do Caramulo, rising to 1,074 meters (3,524 feet) above the ancient town of Viseu, site of a prehistoric settlement around 1900 B.C., stronghold of Viriatus, chief of the Lusitanians, who fought successfully against the invading Romans, and birthplace of Prince Henry the Navigator, who served as the city's first duke. Southeast of the plain rises the steep escarpment of the rugged Serra da Estrela, Portugal's highest mountain range.

The Serra da Estrela, an enormous uplifted block of granite and schist, culminates in 1,993-meter (6,539-foot) Torre. The range is the only one in the country high enough to support typically alpine vegetation on its summits and upper slopes. From its high ridges you look down across steep rocky slopes to pine forests spangled with verdant meadows and small mountain lakes reflecting the sky; into the narrow canyons threaded by the silver bands of boisterous streams tumbling seaward in a series of cascades; and across a panorama of forest, river valleys and fields to the Atlantic, lying beneath a blanket of mist in the distance. Situated at an elevation of 1,056 meters (3,464 feet) on the northeastern slope of the Serra da Estrela is the town of Guarda, capital of Beira Alta. Rising from its sea of red tile roofs is a splendid cathedral of hewn granite, which was begun in 1390 and finished in 1540. The town also boasts an 11th century chapel, 12th century castle and 13th century watchtower. Continuing southwest from the Serra da Estrela are two lesser ranges, the Serra de Açor, rising to 1,409 meters (4,623 feet), and the Serra da Lousã, which attain an elevation of 1,202 meters (3,943 feet). Both ranges are largely covered with pine forests, home of an occasional wolf and wild boar.

Farther south, across the valley of the Rio Zêzere, is a second mountain chain consisting of the Serra de Alvelos, Serra do Muradal and Serra da Gardunha. These ranges look eastward toward Spain over the eroded plateau of Beira Baixa and the ancient provincial capital of Castelo Branco, site of several Roman ruins and a 12th century castle. To the northeast, 42 kilometers from Castelo Branco, is the pre-Roman village of Monsanto, with steep, winding streets flanked by granite houses, some of which are dug into the face of the rocky slope on which the village perches.

The Rio Tejo, which flows westward from Spain to empty into the Atlantic at Lisbon, divides the two provinces of Beira Baixa and Alto Alentejo. Like Baixo Alentejo to the south, Alto Alentejo consists largely of gently rolling hills and vast grasslands interspersed with woodlands of cork and holm oak. Scattered throughout the Alentejo are small villages with white-washed buildings and red tile roofs, each of which seems to have its own medieval castle. You'll find them in Alandroal, Arraiolos, Borba, Estremoz, Évora-Monte, Mourão, Marvão, Portalegre and Vila Viçosa, to name only a few. Near the village of Elvas are the remains of the magnificent Roman aqueduct of Amoreira, with its four arched tiers. The remains of a Roman temple still stand in Évora, the provincial capital. Roman ruins are also located near Tourega, as well as a megalithic dolmen. Near Santiago do Escoural is a system of caves with prehistoric rock paintings. And everywhere there are fabulous churches, some dating back to the 12th and 13th centuries.

Tourist Information

See *Address Directory*:

Comissão Municipal de Turismo de Castelo Branco.
Comissão Municipal de Turismo de Évora.
Comissão Municipal de Turismo da Guarda.
Comissão Municipal de Turismo de Viseu.

Comissão Municipal de Turismo de Serra da Estrela. Offices also in Fundão, Gouveia, Manteigas and Seia.

Tourist offices are also located in several other towns in the region.

Maps

Beira Alta: I.G.C. Carta Corográfica 1:50,000, sheets 13 B and D; 14 A, B, C and D; 15 A, B, C and D; 16 B and D; 17 A, B, C and D; 18 A, B, C and D; 20 A and B; and 21 A and B.

Beira Alta—Serra do Caramulo: I.G.C. Carta Corográfica 1:50,000, sheets 16 B and D; and 17 A and C.

Beira Alta—Serra da Estrela & Serra do Açor: I.G.C. Carta Corográfica 1:50,000, sheets 17 D; 18 C; and 20 A, B, C and D.

Beira Alta—Serra de Montemuro, Serra da Lapa, Serra de Leomil & Serra do Arada: I.G.C. Carta Corográfica 1:50,000, sheets 13 B and D; and 14 A, B, C and D.

Beira Alta—Serra de Marofa & Serra de Malcata: I.G.C. Carta Corográfica 1:50,000, sheets 15 C and D; and 21 A and B.

Beira Baixa: I.G.C. Carta Corográfica 1:50,000, sheets 20 B, C and D; 21 A, C and D; 23 D; 24 A, B, C and D; 25 A, B and C; and 28 A and B.

Beira Baixa—Serra de Alvelos, Serra do Muradel & Serra da Gardunha: I.G.C. Carta Corográfica 1:50,000, sheets 20 C and D; and 24 A, B, C and D.

Alto Alentejo: I.G.C. Carta Corográfica 1:50,000, sheets 28 A, B, C and D; 29 C; 31 B and D; 32 A, B, C and D; 33 A, C and D; 35 B and D; 36 A, B, C and D; 37 A and C; 39 B; 40 A, B, C and D; and 41 A and C.

Alto Alentejo—Serra de Marvão & Serra de São Mamede: I.G.C. Carta Corográfica 1:50,000, sheets 28 D, 29 C, 32 B and 33 A.

Suggested Walking Areas

Some of the finest walking in Portugal is to be found in the mountains of the Beira provinces, especially in the Serra da Estrela. Footpaths and unpaved mountain tracks wind throughout the range, even to the highest peaks and ridges where cross-country walking is possible. You can wander through meadows and forests, along streams, up rocky canyons with waterfalls and beside the shores of high lakes. There are rock walls to climb and, in the winter, snowy slopes for cross-country skiing.

Other ranges to explore include the Serra de Arada, Serra de Leomil and Serra de Montemuro in northwestern Beira Alta; the Serra do Caramulo west of Viseu; the Serra de Marofa and Serra de Malcata in eastern Beira Alta; and the Serra de Alvelos, Serra do Muradal and Serra da Gardunha west of Castelo Branco in Beira Baixa.

There are fewer walking opportunities in Alto Alentejo, although you can always follow lonely country tracks through the woods and grasslands, winding among the hills from town to town. You might also try exploring the Serra de Marvão and Serra de São Mamede along the Spanish frontier.

Beira Litoral, Estremadura & Ribatejo

According to legend, the city of Lisbon was founded by the Greek hero Ulysses. Historians agree that the city dates back to the Homeric era, but attribute its foundation in 1200 B.C. not to the Greeks, but instead to Phoenician traders, who valued its sheltered waters at the mouth of the Rio Tejo. The "Calm Harbor," as they named the settlement, provided welcome moorage in the long journey between the tin mines of Britain and the ancient trading centers of the eastern Mediterranean.

Lying west of the Pillars of Hercules, Lisbon was the last reliable anchorage before setting across the Atlantic to the British Isles. About 25 kilometers west of the city, the ancient ships would round Cabo Rosa, then Cabo Roca, the westernmost point of continental Europe, and from there only open ocean would lie ahead.

After the Phoenicians, the city was successively invaded by the Celts, Romans, Visigoths and Moors. The Moors remained in the city for four centuries until 1147 when Dom Afonso Henriques, the first king of Portugal, captured it with the aid of the Crusaders. A little more than a century later, it replaced Coimbra as the capital of the newly formed kingdom. Set on seven hills, Lisbon is today a city of spacious, tree-lined avenues with sidewalks of black and white cobblestones laid in intricate patterns, arcaded buildings, ancient ruins and the *Alfama,* a hilly quarter of narrow, winding streets that climb steeply between old balconied buildings draped with laundry drying in the sun, site of Roman and Moorish Lisbon.

From Cabo Roca west of Lisbon, Portugal's central coast—the Costa de Prata—extends northward for more than 125 kilometers to the city of Porto, at the mouth of Rio Douro. The southern half of this coast lies in the province of Estremadura, the northern half in the province of Beira Litoral. Along its length are rocky headlands, golden strands, great stretches of sand dunes, large estuaries and lagoons. In several places, such as near Leiria and Aveiro, pine forests extend nearly to the shore. The forest of Marinha Grande above Leiria, Portugal's largest, was first planted in the 13th and 14th centuries to stabilize the coastal dunes and thus allow the development of agriculture in the immediate hinterlands. The dunes are the highest in Europe.

Coastal woodlands are typical of northern Estremadura and Beira Litoral, but in southern Estremadura the sea bluffs and coastal hills are more often covered by a dense mantle of scrub. Brush pungent with rosemary and thyme also grows on the rolling hills of the hinterland, such as near the shrine of Fátima, along with oak woodlands and stands of pine.

Estuaries and lagoons, often bordered by wooded dunes, occur along the coast where rivers empty into the sea. The largest lagoon is located at the mouth of the Rio Vouga, near the town of Aveiro. It is contained behind two wooded sandpits and includes several islands and winding channels. Plying the sheltered waters are the distinctive low-slung craft known as *moliceiros,* with their single sails and high, curved prows festively decorated with folk motifs. Used for harvesting seaweed in the lagoon, these distinctive craft ride so low in the water that from a distance the midship gunwales seem nearly submerged.

The Costa de Prata is bordered by rolling, sandy hills, basalt plateaus and steep escarpments of sandstone and limestone. In places the hills drop suddenly to the sea. Just as often they give way to narrow, uplifted coastal plains that terminate in precipitous sea bluffs. The spectacular effects of wave erosion are best exhibited at Cabo Carvoeiro and Berlenga island, where caves, arches and narrow defiles have been carved into the coastal cliffs.

The hinterland is a region of rugged hills, scarplands and plateaus deeply dissected by streams. Pine forests, oak woodlands and scrub form a varied vegetation mosaic on the slopes, while the valleys are usually open and cultivated. The Serra do Buçaco, north of the town of Coimbra, is heavily wooded with both pines and hardwoods and contains several springs. Other ranges include the Serra da Lousã, which attains an elevation of 1,204 meters (3,950 feet), the Serra de Sicó, the Serra de Candeeiros and the Serra de Montejunto.

East of the coastal hinterland, rugged terrain gives way to the broad lowland of Ribatejo, which embraces the lower reaches of the Rio Tejo. This gentle basin, formed from the sediments deposited by its great river, is a vast pastureland, where herds of wild cattle range over the grasslands with sheep and horses.

As in the rest of Portugal, the Costa de Prata and Ribatejo are characterized by numerous charming towns and villages nestled among the hills, along the coast and on the open plains. The fewest settlements are found in the Ribatejo which contains only one sizable town—Santarém—and a few widely scattered farming communities. Along the coast, there are numerous fishing villages as well as bustling resort centers with luxurious hotels. Chief among the many coastal resorts is Estoril, west of Lisbon, which has a plush casino surrounded by lovely gardens. Of the fishing villages, one of the most notable is Nazaré, situated on a sandy beach at the foot of a 110-meter promontory, where the men normally wear checkered trousers and shirts and long black woolen caps, and the women wear seven skirts or petticoats of a different color and flat black hats with a brim.

If possible, there are even more castles, medieval churches, Roman ruins and other historical monuments in Estremadura and Beira Litoral than elsewhere in Portugal. And you find them not only in Lisbon and the larger towns, but in just about every village. Rare is the community that doesn't have one or more historical monuments. Among the more notable are the 8th century Moorish castle at Sintra, the 12th century Templar castle at Tomar, the 13th century university buildings of Coimbra, the Roman ruins of Conímbriga, the marvelous twin-spired castle of Porto de Mós, the Marmaltar megaliths near Aveiro, the castle and crenelated walls of Obidos, and the castle of St. George in Lisbon.

Tourist Information

See *Address Directory*:

Comissão Municipal de Turismo de Lisboa.

Comissão Municipal de Turismo de Santarém.

Comissão Municipal de Turismo de Aveiro.

Comissão Regional de Turismo de Leiria. Offices also in Fátima, Monte Real, Praia de Pedrógão, Vieira de Leiria, Batalha, Mira de Aire, Vila Nova de Ourém, S. Pedro de Muel and Porto de Mós.

Comissão Regional de Turismo da Serra da Arrábida. Offices also in Sesimbra and Palmela.

Other tourist offices are found in towns throughout the region.

Maps

Beira Litoral: I.G.C. Carta Corográfica 1:50,000, sheets 13 A, B, C and D; 16 A, B, C and D; 19 A, B, C and D; 20 A and C; 22 B and D; 23 A, B, C and D; 24 A; and 27 A.

Beira Litoral—Rio Vouga to Rio Mondego: I.G.C. Carta Corográfica 1:50,000, sheets 16 A and C; and 19 A and C.

Beira Litoral—Serra do Buçaco & Serra da Lousã: I.G.C. Carta Corográfica 1:50,000, sheets 19 B and D; 20 C; 23 B; and 24 A.

Estremadura: I.G.C. Carta Corográfica 1:50,000, sheets 22 D; 26 B, C and D; 27 A; 30 A, B, C and D; 34 A, B, C and D; 35 A and C; 38 B; and 39 A.

Estremadura—Serra da Arrábida, Cabo Espichel & Sesimbra: I.G.C. Carta Corográfica 1:50,000, sheets 34 D and 38 B.

Estremadura—Coastal Walk: I.G.C. Carta Corográfica 1:50,000, sheets 30 A and C; and 34 A and C.

Estremadura—Serra Montejunto: I.G.C. Carta Corográfica 1:50,000, sheets 30 B and D.

Estremadura—Serra de Candeeiros & Serra de Aire (Porto de Mós): I.G.C. Carta Corográfica 1:50,000, sheets 26 B and D; and 27 A and C.

Ribatejo: I.G.C. Carta Corográfica 1:50,000, sheets 27 A, B, C and D; 28 A and C; 30 B and D; 31 A, B, C and D; 34 B; and 35 A and B.

Suggested Walking Areas

Several fine walks are possible within only a few kilometers of Lisbon. For spectacular views of the sea, ramble from summit to summit along the gentle ridgecrest of the Serra da Arrábida, a limestone massif rising to 501 meters (1,644 feet) on the precipitous southern shore of the Setúbal Peninsula south of the city. For an even closer look at the ocean, you can walk the coast at the foot of the range. Heading either direction from the town of Sesimbra, you can follow footpaths and unpaved tracks along the sea bluffs. From the rocky headland of Cabo Espichel, it is possible to walk north, mostly along beaches, to the sandy point across the Rio Tejo from the Lisbon coast, a distance of about 30 kilometers.

The Lisbon coast is intensely developed and therefore offers limited walking opportunities. But a few kilometers to the west, where the coast turns northward at Cabo Raso, you can stroll along the lonely bluffs and beaches of the Costa de Prata for some distance, following footpaths, unpaved tracks and your own instincts.

The Beira Litoral offers fine coastal walks through dunes, along sandy beaches and by lovely lagoons. One possibility is to head south from the mouth of the Rio Vouga just north of Aveiro to Figueira da Foz at the mouth of the Rio Mondego. This section of coast is largely undeveloped and only occasionally visited by major roads. The entire route covers about 50 kilometers.

If you prefer hill walking, the coastal hinterland provides numerous opportunities. Among the areas worth exploring are the Serra do Buçaco, Serra da Lousã and the hill country surrounding Porto de Mós.

Minho, Douro Litoral, Trás Os Montes & Alto Douro

These four provinces comprise the northernmost part of Portugal. They are bounded on the south by Beira Litoral and Beira Alta, and on the north by Spain. Porto, Portugal's second largest city, sits near the mouth of the Rio Douro in the southern part of the Douro Litoral. The northern provinces are the coolest and wettest in the country, receiving significantly more rain, especially during the summer, than those farther south. They are excellent places to walk during the midsummer, when the heat of the south may be prohibitive.

Minho, in the extreme northwestern corner of Portugal, is a mountainous region, with several ranges rising above 1,200 meters. Among these are the Serra da Peneda (1,373 meters; 4,504 feet) and Serra do Gerês (1,508 meters; 4,947 feet), both situated in the Parque Nacional de Peneda-Gerês, and the Serra da Cabreira (1,262 meters; 4,140 feet) on the southern border of the park. Lower ranges cover virtually all the rest of the region, where just about the only gentle terrain lies at the bottom of narrow, steep-walled river valleys. The gorges of the Rio Lima and Rio Cávado are especially notable.

The Minho coastal strip is relatively narrow, rising quickly to foothills more than 400 meters (1,312 feet) high. Dense oak woodland and pine forest form a verdant mantle over much of the province, which receives more rainfall than any other in Portugal. Numerous streams tumble through the forest and beautiful reservoirs surrounded by woods lie among the hills.

The terrain and vegetation of the Douro Litoral, which borders Minho on the south, is much the same, except that there are fewer ranges exceeding 1,200 meters. The highest are the Serra de Alvão (1,285 meters; 4,216 feet) and the Serra do Marão (1,415 meters; 4,642 feet).

East of Minho and Douro Litoral, the Trás-os-Montes and Alto Douro provinces extend east to the Spanish frontier. This region consists of a high, partly broken tableland composed of Precambrian granites, schists and slates. This plateau has been cut in places by narrow river gorges up to 488 meters (1,600 feet) deep. It is surmounted in the north by the Serra do Larouco (1,527 meters; 5,010 feet), Serra da Coroa (1,272 meters; 4,173 feet) and Serra de Montezinho (1,273 meters; 4,176 feet); and in the east by the Serra de Nogueira (1,318 meters; 4,324 feet), Serra de Bornes (1,174 meters; 3,852 feet) and Serra de Mogadouro (995 meters; 3,264 feet)—all of which are remnants of extremely ancient mountain ranges. There are also two ranges—the Serra do Barroso (1,279 meters; 4,196 feet) and Serra da Padrela (1,148 meters; 3,766 feet)—southwest of the town of Chaves. Like the uplands of Beira Alta to the south, the tableland of Trás-os-Montes and Alto Douro is a westward extension of Spain's Meseta plateau.

Notable among the historic monuments of northern Portugal are the 12th century cathedral at Braga; the walled town of Bragança, with its 12th century castle; the Roman bridge at Chaves; and the lovely Gothic monastery at Matosinhos. Numerous other castles, cathedrals, chapels, ruins and the like are scattered throughout the North.

Tourist Information

See *Address Directory*:

Comissão Municipal de Turismo de Viana do Castelo.

Comissão Municipal de Turismo do Porto.

Comissão Municipal de Turismo de Bragança.

Comissão Regional de Turismo de Chaves. Offices also in Termas and Vidago.

Comissão Regional de Turismo da Serra do Marão. Office also in Amarante.

Other tourist offices are found in towns throughout the region.

Maps

Douro Litoral: I.G.C. Carta Corográfica 1:50,000, sheets 9 A, B, C and D; 10 A and C; 13 A and B; and 14 A.

Douro Litoral—Serra de Alvão & Serra do Marão: I.G.C. Carta Corográfica 1:50,000, sheets 9 B and D; and 10 A and C.

Minho: I.G.C. Carta Corográfica 1:50,000, sheets 1 A, B, C and D; 2 C; 5 A, B, C and D; 6 A and C; and 9 A.

Minho—Serra da Peneda, Serra do Suajo, Serra da Cabreira & Serra do

Gerês: I.G.C. Carta Corográfica 1:50,000, sheets 1 D; 2 C; 5 B and D; 6 A and C.

Minho & Douro Litoral—Costa Verde: I.G.C. Carta Corográfica 1:50,000, sheets 1 C; 5 A and C; and 9 A and C.

Trás-os-Montes & Alto Douro: I.G.C. Carta Corográfica 1:50,000, sheets 2 C and D; 3 C and D; 4 C; 6 A, B, C and D; 7 A, B, C and D; 8 A and C; 10 A, B, C and D; 11 A, B, C and D; 12 A; and 15 A and B.

Trás-os-Montes & Alto Douro—Serra do Larouco: I.G.C. Carta Corográfica 1:50,000, sheets 2 C and D; and 6 A and B.

Trás-os-Montes & Alto Douro—Serra da Coroa, Serra de Montezinho, Serra da Nogueira & Serra de Bornes: I.G.C. Carta Corográphica 1:50,000, sheets 3 C and D; 7 A, B, C and D; and 11 A and B.

Suggested Walking Areas

The mountain ranges of the northern provinces offer excellent walking. Most are covered by fairly extensive networks of footpaths linking the villages on opposite sides of the ranges. In the Serra da Peneda and Serra do Gerês in particular, the paths can be linked up to form long excursions. This feature, combined with the region's beautiful forests, gorges, lakes and streams, makes the North one of the finest places to walk in Portugal. In few other regions is it possible to plan such extended mountain walks. In addition to the two ranges mentioned above, the following also offer excellent possibilities: the Serra de Alvão and Serra do Marão in Douro Litoral, and the Serra do Larouco and Serra da Nogueira in Trás-os-Montes and Alto Douro. It is also possible to walk along the Costa Verde.

Address Directory

A

- *Associação Portuguesa de Pousadas de juventude,* 46 Rua Andrade Corvo, P-1000 Lisboa. Tel. 57 10 54.

C

- *Caminhos de Ferro Portugueses:* Tel. Lisbon 32 62 26 or 32 62 27.
- *Casa Senna,* Rua Nova do Almada 48/52, P-1200 Lisboa. Tel. 32 34 37.
- *Casa Socidel,* Rua Nova do Almada 47/9, P-1200 Lisboa. Tel. 32 60 46 or 32 77 68.
- *Clube Nacional de Montanhismo,* Rua Formosa 303, Porto. Tel. 28 3 23.

- Comissão Municipal de Turismo da Guarda, Praça Luis de Camões, Edificio da Câmara, Guarda. Tel. 22 2 51.
- Comissão Municipal de Turismo de Aveiro, Praça da República, Aveiro. Tel. 23 6 80.
- Comissão Municipal de Turismo de Beja, Rua Capitão João Francisco Sousa 25, Beja. Tel. 23 6 93.
- Comissão Municipal de Turismo de Bragança, Avenida 25 de Abril, Bragança. Tel. 22 2 71.
- Comissão Municipal de Turismo de Castelo Branco, Alameda da Liberdade, Castelo Branco. Tel. 10 02.
- Comissão Municipal de Turismo de Évora, Praça do Giraldo 71, Évora. Tel. 22 6 71.
- Comissão Municipal de Turismo de Lisboa, 141 Rua Portas de St. Antão. P-1100, Lisboa. Tel. 36 66 24.
- Comissão Municipal de Turismo de Santarém, Edificio da Câmara, Santarém. Tel. 22 1 30.
- Comissão Municipal de Turismo de Serra da Estrela, Praça do Municipio, Covilhã. Tel. 22 1 70.
- Comissão Municipal de Turismo de Viana do Castelo, Avenida Cândido dos Reis, Palácio dos Távoras, Viana do Castelo. Tel. 22 6 20.
- Comissão Municipal de Turismo de Viseu, Avenida Gulbenkian, Viseu. Tel. 22 2 94.
- Comissão Municipal de Turismo do Porto, Praça Gen. Humberto Delgado, Porto. Tel. 29 8 71 or 31 27 40.
- Comissão Regional de Turismo da Serra da Arrábida, Largo do Corpo Santo, Setúbal. Tel. 24 2 84 and 24 2 04.
- Comissão Regional de Turismo da Serra do Marão, Avenida Carvalho Araújo, Vila Real. Tel. 22 8 19.
- Comissão Regional de Turismo de Chaves, Rua de St. António 213, Chaves. Tel. 29.
- Comissão Regional de Turismo de Leiria, Largo Gôa, Damão e Diu, Leiria. Tel. 22 7 48.
- Comissão Regional de Turismo do Algarve, Rua Ataíde de Oliveira 100, Faro. Tel. 24 0 67 or 24 0 68.

D

- da Silva, F. Pires and A. Almeida Henriques, Rua Manuel Lirio 2, R/C.-Esq.·, Amadora.
- Direcção-Geral do Turismo, Avenida António Augusto de Aguiar 86, apartado 1929, P-1099 Lisboa. Tel. 57 50 86.

E

- *Editorial de Publicações Turisticas,* Rua de Santa Barbara 81, 5.·-D, P-1100 Lisboa. Tel. 53 44 96.
- *Emergency:* Tel. 115.

F

- *F. Pires da Silva,* see *da Silva, F. Pires.*

I

- *Instituto Geográfico e Cadastral,* Venda de Cartas, Praça da Estrela, P-1200 Lisboa. Tel. 61 61 75.

M

- *Marcampo,* Avenida Almirante Gago Coutinho 56 D, P-1700 Lisboa. Tel. 88 67 76 or 89 65 79.

P

- *Portuguese National Tourist Office, London,* New Bond Street House, 1st Floor Suite, 1/5 New Bond Street, London W1Y OBD. Tel. (01) 493 3873.
- *Portuguese National Tourist Office, New York,* 548 Fifth Avenue, New York, New York 10036. Tel. (212) 354-4403.

S

- *Solecampo.* Avenida Sacadura Cabral 22 B, P-1000 Lisboa. Tel. 76 02 48.

T

- *Tecnicampo Lda.,* 44 Avenida Alm. Reis, P-1100 Lisboa. Tel. 82 22 87.

W

- *Weather:* Instituto Nacional de Meteorologia e Geofisica. Tel. 80 21 19.

A Quick Reference

In a hurry? Turn to the pages listed below. They will give you the most important information on walking in Portugal.

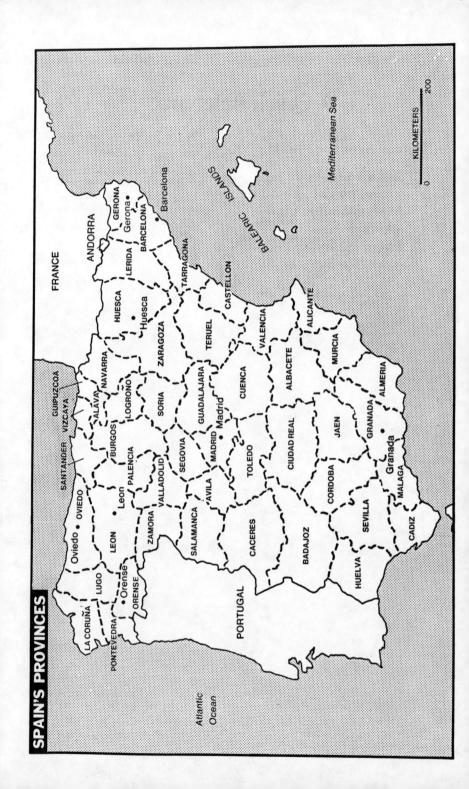

SPAIN'S PROVINCES

Spain

THE SPAIN OF imagination is a land of Moorish castles, flamenco dancers, bullfights, the windmills of La Mancha and the conuistadores. It is a country rich in the art of such masters as El Greco, Velazquez, Goya and Picasso. Tourist brochures glory in the golden plains and hills of central Spain, in the wealth of sunny beaches that draw hundreds of thousands of visitors each year to Spain's rocky coasts and in the historic and architectural treasures of cities such as Avila, Granada, Barcelona, Madrid, Segovia and Valladolid.

Yet there is another Spain that is less well known—the Spain of lofty mountain crests crowned with pinnacles and snow, of high lakes fringed with verdant meadows or forests of pine, fir, beech and oak. This is the Spain of walkers, where lonely footpaths wind through rugged gorges, past tumbling waters and mountain tarns, across high barren plateaus and over rugged crests shared with ibex and moufflon sheep.

In fact, Spain is one of the most mountainous countries in Europe, with an average elevation second only to that of Switzerland. In addition to the famed Pyrenees, which straddle the border with France, four other great mountain chains extend for hundreds of kilometers across the country. All offer a wealth of walking and cross-country skiing opportunities amid scenery to rival that of the Alps.

No one knows just how many kilometers of footpaths exist in Spain, but the figure surely must be counted in the tens of thousands. Most of the paths are unmarked, but for most mountain regions there are a variety of map-guides and a lesser number of guidebooks to help you find your way. In addition, courteous and hospitable villagers are often more than glad to direct you along the proper paths—and to engage in a moment of animated banter.

It is possible to walk throughout most of Spain, but away from the mountain ranges little information is available. There are thousands of kilometers of rural paths and wagon tracks, however, to take you away from the busy highways and crowded centers of tourism.

Spain is the third largest country in Europe, with a total area of over 500,000 square kilometers (193,000 square miles). More than 60 percent of this area is dominated by the great central plateau—the *Meseta*—with an average elevation of more than 610 meters (2,000 feet) and steep, eroded, reddish slopes which recall the American West. Bounded on the west by Portugal and on the other three sides by mountain ranges, it is a sparsely populated region where many a village stands nearly empty with tile roofs fallen in and adobe washing away—victims of the exodus of youth who have gone to Spain's cities to find better-paying jobs.

On the north, the Meseta ends at the foothills of the Cordillera Cantabrica, which extends along Spain's northern coast from the Basque provinces in the east to Galicia in the west. This complex system of ranges contains many peaks rising above over 2,500 meters (8,200 feet), including the three massifs of the Picos de Europa, one of Spain's most spectacular mountain districts. North of the mountains lies the narrow coastal plain of Cantabria, where waves crash against pine-topped rocks guarding curved beaches.

The Meseta is bounded on the east by the Sistema Ibérico, a lower mountain chain made up of numerous ranges, only a few of which top 2,000 meters (6,562 feet). From the provinces of Burgos and Logroño in the north, the Sistema Ibérico extends southwest toward Valencia and the Costa del Azahar—the Coast of Orange Blossoms—and is the source of two of the three great rivers of Castile, the Río Duero in the north and the Río Tajo in the south.

The Sistema Central, which consists largely of two major ranges, the Sierra de Gredos and Sierra de Guadarrama, extends southwestward from the Sistema Ibérico across the Meseta into Extremadura, the arid, sparsely populated land of Spain's great explorers and conquistadors—Cortés and Pizarro, Balboa and Orellana, Pedro de Alvarado and Hernando de Soto. The Sistema Central divides the Meseta into two parts: Old Castile to the north and New Castile to the south. Madrid, Spain's capital and largest city, lies in New Castile only a few dozen kilometers south of the mountains. With rugged peaks rising to more than 2,500 meters (8,200 feet) elevation, these ranges offer excellent walking and skiing within an hour's drive from the city.

South of Madrid stretches the barren tableland of La Mancha with its fabled windmills and the lingering ghost of Don Quixote. Across the plateau flows the Río Guadiana, the longest river in Spain, which rises in the Sistema Penibético and flows westward into Portugal.

The Sistema Penibético is the longest and highest of Spain's mountain systems, and along with the rugged hills of the Sierra Morena forms the southern boundary of the Meseta. Its greatest range, the Sierra Nevada, closely parallels the Costa del Sol south of Granada, where vineyards grow grapes for sherry in the province of Cadiz and whitewashed hill towns overlook meadows raising fighting bulls. Within the Sierra Nevada rise the two highest peaks in the Iberian Peninsula: Mulhacen (3,481 meters; 11,420 feet) and Veleta (3,428 meters; 11,246 feet). The city of Granada, with the romantic Moorish palace of the Alhambra, lies at the northern foot of the mountains. North of the Sierra Nevada, in Jaen province, is the Sierra de Cazorla, a much lower range, but one which is rich in plants and animals and offers excellent walking.

East of the Sistema Ibérico, lies the valley of the Río Ebro, which flows through Navarre and Aragon and forms the southern boundary of

Catalunya. All three regions are bounded on the north by the Pyrenees, which are neither the longest nor highest mountain range in Spain, but offer the most extensive array of high peaks in the country. The Pyrenees also contain the most mountain refuges and ski areas and the greatest network of footpaths of any of the Spanish ranges.

Scattered across Spain's convoluted terrain is a wealth of historical treasures—the 12,000-year-old cave paintings at Altamira; Celtic cromlechs and Iberian remains; Romanesque churches; Roman theaters and aqueducts; the horseshore arches and slender towers of Moorish mosques and palaces; and lonely castles attesting to the waves of Crusaders who, on and off for more than 750 years, successively pushed Islam south and finally removed Moorish rule from Spain in 1492. Spain is a land of diverse peoples, cultures and landscapes which history has divided into many distinct and fiercely individualistic regions. By simply crossing one of the Spanish mountain ranges, you sometimes feel you are in another country. One leading newspaper even talks of 15 Spains, a nation of nations. The official language is Castilian Spanish, but it is by no means Spain's only language. The language of Catalunya, Valencia and the Balearic Islands to the east is Catalan. In the Basque provinces of northeastern Spain you encounter the ancient language of Euskara, and in Spain's northwestern corner the everyday language is Gallego. Most printed walking information is in Spanish, but the walker in northern and eastern Spain must also use map-guides and guidebooks in Catalan. If you speak Spanish, you will have few problems communicating with local people. Many educated Spaniards also speak French. But in some villages the second language is Spanish and if you don't speak it you must resort to sign language in order to communicate.

Flora & Fauna

Spain has an extraordinary variety of plants, including types characteristic of such climatically different regions as the British highlands, Central Europe and North Africa. The mountains are frequently forested on their lower slopes with pines and junipers, which give way at higher elevations to meadows and alpine communities. The forests of the Pyrenees also contain silver fir, as well as such hardwoods as beech, birch and hazel, trees that are absent from the southern ranges.

In more arid regions the forest gives way to woodlands of evergreen oaks and holly, interspersed with stands of drought resistant scrub known as *matorral*. In the driest areas, such as the plains of La Mancha, vast areas are covered by annual grasses and herbs that are verdant during the winter and spring, but turn to gold during the summer months.

The Spanish mountains are rich in big game, including wild boar, lynx, roe and fallow deer, chamoix, ibex, and moufflon sheep. Wolves are occasionally seen in the northern ranges. There is a small population of bears in the Pyrenees. The country contains numerous wildlife reserves intended to protect habitats and regulate hunting practices. These include 6 national parks, 36 national reserves, 850 big game reserves and thousands of private reserves. Hunting is strictly forbidden in the national parks except to regulate game populations. Spain has fixed hunting seasons, which are varied from year to year according to environmental factors and species populations. Walkers who wish to avoid certain areas during peak hunting times should first consult local residents, or local offices of ICONA (Instituto Nacional Para la Conservación de la Naturaleza).

Spain does not have a great variety of small land birds. Quail, grouse, pheasants and partridges, however, are found throughout the country. Eagles, hawks and vultures are also fairly common in the mountains. A great variety of waterfowl and wading birds frequent Spanish marshes and coasts during the winter. The great marshes of the Río Guadalquivir, southwest of Sevilla, are known to ornithologists the world over for the astounding numbers and varieties of birds to be found there. These include flamingos, spoonbills, geese, ducks and numerous species common to North Africa. The Guadalquivir marshes are now protected in the Parque Nacional de Doñana.

Snakes include the poisonous viper, which is fairly common in some areas, and the boa constrictor, which is extremely rare and confined to the extreme south. Neither snake presents much of a problem to walkers, although a bite from the viper should receive immediate medical attention. In midsummer, mosquitoes can be bothersome in marshy areas, such as the delta of the Río Ebro on Catalunya's Costa Dorada. Mosquitoes may also be encountered near some mountain lakes. Although their numbers are usually few, a mosquito repellent will make the evening hours more pleasant.

Climate

The climate of Spain varies greatly from region to region, largely because its numerous mountain ranges interrupt and divert the normal flow of air masses over the peninsula. As a rule, however, summers tend to be hot and dry and winters cool and moist over most of the country. Such a climate is typical of the Mediterranean region.

Rainfall is greatest in the northwest and along the Cantabrian coast in the north, where rain, drizzle and mist are frequent even in midsummer. Santander, for example, receives measurable precipitation nearly 200 days a year. A dramatic contrast is provided by Spain's southern coast, where even the lofty Sierra Nevada boasts some 250 days of sunshine per year. The Meseta receives scant rainfall the year round. What little it does get falls mostly in the spring with March and April being the wettest months.

Snowfall covers the Spanish mountains from November to June and sometimes remains later in a few of the higher, chillier locations. The lower limit of the snowpack is about 1,800 meters in the Sierra Nevada in extreme southern Spain, but drops significantly lower in the northern ranges. Although most of higher ranges in Spain show signs of extensive former glaciation, there is no longer any perennial ice in the country.

The Meseta experiences wide extremes of temperature over the course of the year. In Madrid, for example, the average low temperature for January is 2°C. (36°F.) and the average high for July is 31°C. (88°F.).

The provinces of Sevilla and Cordoba, in southwestern Spain, are the hottest in the country. In Cordoba, for instance, the average high temperature in July is 37°C. (99°F.). The coldest places in the country are Avila, Albacete, Burgos, León and Soria, all located in mountainous districts. In Avila, 112 kilometers northwest of Madrid, for example, the average daily low in January is *minus* 2°C. (28°F.); the average high, only 7°C. (45°F.).

Weather Forecasts

You can obtain weather information for any region in Spain by telephoning:

Centro de Análisis y Predicción (Ciudad Universitaria), Tel. (91) 244 35 00. Staff speaks Spanish.

When asking for information, be sure to specify the region in which you are interested and what type of information you desire—temperatures, rainfall, winds and so on.

When in Madrid, you can obtain a local recorded forecast in Spanish by telephoning: Tel. 094.

For all other parts of Spain, you can obtain a recorded forecast by telephoning: Tel. (91) 232 35 00.

Where to Get Walking Information

Attempting to obtain walking information for Spain prior to your arrival in the country can be a frustrating, often fruitless experience. First, there is no central source of walking information for the entire country. Instead, you are faced with an array of regional and provincial mountaineering federations, each with a number of affiliated clubs. To obtain information on a particular walking area, you must write the appropriate federation or even one or more of its local clubs. Second, even if you know where you want to walk and have obtained the address of the appropriate clubs, there is no guarantee your enquiries will be answered. The Spanish are a friendly, hospitable, altogether enjoyable people, but their attitude toward correspondence—indeed, business in general—is sometimes rather casual by general European standards.

To increase your chances of receiving a reply, you should:

1. Write to the appropriate provincial mountaineering federation for the area in which you wish to walk (the addresses of the federations are listed in the *Address Directory* at the end of this chapter);
2. Write several months in advance to allow time for slow mail delivery and follow-up letters;
3. Write only in Spanish; letters written in other languages are unlikely to be answered; there is no guarantee even for letters in Spanish;
4. Avoid asking questions calling for formal, written replies; it is best to limit correspondence to requests for lists of publications, mountain refuges and activities; schedules of walking and climbing excursions; applications for membership; information on where to obtain refuge keys; and orders for publications supplied by the club;
5. If you don't receive a reply within a reasonable period, send a follow-up letter; if information is still not forthcoming, you might try a second follow-up letter or just forget the whole thing and reconcile yourself to obtaining information after you have arrived in Spain.

In fact, the best way to plan trips in Spain is to obtain the necessary guidebooks and maps and to plan walks on your own, without depending upon the clubs for information. If possible, however, you should make all arrangements for climbing courses, guide services, participating in walking and climbing excursions, and picking up keys to refuges (where necessary) before arriving in Spain—and all these things must be done through the clubs.

Once you are in Spain, of course, you can visit the clubs in person. This is the best way to obtain information from them. Club members are extremely cordial to foreign visitors and will provide whatever assistance they can.

If you are in Madrid, you can also visit the offices of the Federación Española de Montañismo (F.E.M.), to which all provincial mountaineering federations and local clubs belong. The F.E.M. sells several useful publications, can provide the addresses of affiliated clubs and can answer questions about walking in the Sierra de Gredos and Sierra de Guadarrama, the ranges immediately west and north of the city. If you ask for information about walking areas in other parts of Spain, however, the F.E.M. staff will simply direct you to the appropriate regional federations and local clubs.

Most of the Spanish walking clubs have evening office hours. They open at 7 p.m. and close at 9 or 9:30 p.m., just before dinner. (The Spanish dinner hour begins at 10 p.m.) Be sure to call ahead of time to ensure someone is in the office.

Spain's Walking Clubs

Spain has a large, well-developed network of more than 700 walking and mountaineering clubs, with a total of 76,000 members. All the clubs are affiliated with:

Federación Española de Montañismo (for its address and telephone number, see the *Address Directory* at the end of this chapter). Staff speaks Spanish, French and some English.

The F.E.M. is made up of 13 regional and provincial mountaineering federations, each of which includes numerous affiliated local clubs.

Through its regional sections and national committees, the F.E.M. supervises all organized mountaineering activities in Spain. Separate F.E.M. national committees have been established to oversee: 1) long-distance footpaths, 2) mountain refuges, 3) organized membership outings, 4) mountaineering expeditions in Spain and abroad, 5) ski mountaineering, 6) cave exploration and 7) mountaineering for young people. In addition, the F.E.M. supervises the national mountaineering school and the society of mountain guides. Useful publications include:

• *F.E.M. Annuario* (in Spanish). This annual directory is a valuable resource for walkers, listing the addresses and phone numbers of regional and provincial mountaineering federations and their affiliated local clubs, as well as the locations and ownership of all mountain refuges in Spain. If unable to obtain a copy of your own, you can examine one at the F.E.M. office in Madrid or at the offices of the regional and provincial federations.

Membership in the F.E.M. is necessary to participate in its organized activities, which include climbing courses, walking tours and mountaineering expeditions. You must also be an F.E.M. member to use many of the mountain huts owned by its federations and affiliated clubs.

In order to become an F.E.M. member, you must join one of its mountaineering federations or affiliated local clubs. The local clubs organize campouts, walking tours, climbs, ski tours, caving expeditions and other activities. Many operate their own mountain huts and some publish magazines with articles of interest to walkers and climbers. Many of the map-guides and guidebooks to the mountains of Spain are also written and/or published by the local clubs. Activity calendars for all these organizations are available from the appropriate regional and provincial mountaineering federations.

Membership in one F.E.M. affiliated club allows you to participate in organized activities sponsored by any of the F.E.M. clubs and to use club huts anywhere in Spain. In addition, you receive the following benefits:

1. Comprehensive accident insurance, which covers the complete costs of search and rescue and even includes the costs of surgery, if necessary; it also covers the costs of search and rescue in other countries;

2. Discounted rates for the use of F.E.M. mountain refuges;

3. The use of refuges abroad operated by the alpine clubs in Austria, Germany, France, Italy, Switzerland and Luxembourg, as well as by the French Mountaineering Federation and the Camping Club of Lisbon;

4. A card permitting the bearer free access across the border between France and Spain when walking in the Pyrenees; and

5. Special discounts on rail travel and other services.

The regional and provincial mountaineering federations can provide information on walking, climbing, ski mountaineering and cave exploration in their respective regions. They can also provide information on the mountain refuges in their regions, and on walking and climbing tours, mountaineering courses and other activities organized by their affiliated clubs. The federations are:

See Address Directory:

Federación Andaluza de Montañismo. Oversees mountaineering activities in Andalusia (comprised of the provinces of Almeria, Cádiz, Córdoba, Granada, Huelva, Jaen, Málaga, and Sevilla) in southwestern Spain, including the Sistema Pentibético and Sierra Nevada. Affiliated with 62 local clubs devoted to mountaineering and cave exploration. Staff speaks Spanish.

Federación Aragonesa de Montañismo. Oversees mountaineering activities in Aragon (comprised of the provinces of Huesca, Teruel and Zaragoza) in northeastern Spain, including the Sistema Ibérico and the central Pyrenees. Affiliated with 30 local clubs devoted to mountaineering, cave exploration and other activities. Staff speaks Spanish.

Federación Asturiana de Montañismo. Oversees mountaineering activities in Asturias (comprised of the province of Oviedo) on Spain's northern coast, including the western ranges of the Cordillera Cantábrica and the Picos de Europa. Affiliated with 41 local clubs devoted to mountaineering and skiing. Staff speaks Spanish.

Federación Canaria de Montañismo. Oversees mountaineering activities in the eastern portion of the Canary Islands off the coast of Africa. Affiliated with seven local clubs devoted to mountaineering. Staff speaks Spanish.

Federación Castellana de Montañismo. Oversees mountaineering activities in Castile (comprised of the provinces of Avila, Badajos, Burgos, Cáceres, Ciudad Real, Cuenca, Guadalajara, Logroño, Madrid, Salamanca, Segovia, Soria, Toledo, Valladolid and Zamora) in central Spain, including the Sistema Ibérico and the Sierra de Gredos and Sierra de Guadarrama in the Sistema Central. Affiliated with 153 local clubs devoted to mountaineering, cave exploration and other activities. Staff speaks Spanish. A few staff members also speak some French and English.

Federació d'Entitats Excursionistes de Catalunya (Federación Catalana de Montañismo). Oversees mountaineering activities in Catalunya (comprised of the provinces of Barcelona, Gerona, Lérida and Tarragona) in northeastern Spain, including the eastern Pyrenees. Affiliated with 145 local clubs devoted to mountaineering, skiing and other activities. Staff speaks Catalan and Spanish.

Federación Gallega de Montañismo. Oversees mountaineering activities in Galicia (comprised of the provinces of La Coruña, Lugo, Orense and Pontevedra) in northwestern Spain, including the Sierra and Picos de Ancares in the Montañas Galaicas. Affiliated with 19 local mountaineering clubs. Staff speaks Gallego and Spanish.

Federación Leonesa de Montañismo. Oversees mountaineering activities in the province of León, including the western ranges of the Cordillera Cantábrica and the Picos de Europa. Affiliated with 18 local clubs devoted to mountaineering and cave exploration. Staff speaks Spanish.

Federación Palentina de Montañismo. Oversees mountaineering activities in the province of Palencia in north-central Spain, including the Cordillera Cantábrica and Picos de Europa. Affiliated with 14 local clubs devoted to mountaineering and cave exploration. Staff speaks Spanish.

Federación Tinerfeña de Montañismo. Oversees mountaineering activities in the western portion of the Canary Islands off the coast of Africa. Affiliated with 10 local clubs devoted to mountaineering. Staff speaks Spanish.

Federación Valenciana de Montañismo. Oversees mountaineering activities in the provinces of Albacete, Alicante, Castellón, Murcia and Valencia on Spain's Mediterranean coast, including the southern ranges of the Sistema Ibérico. Affiliated with 41 local clubs devoted to mountaineering, cave exploration and other activities. Staff speaks Catalan and Spanish.

Federación Vasco-Navarra de Montañismo. Oversees mountaineering activities in the Basque provinces of Vizcaya, Guipúzcoa and Alava, as well as in the province of Navarra, including the Western Pyrenees and the easternmost portion of the Cordillera Cantábrica. Affiliated with 145 local clubs devoted to mountaineering, skiing, cave exploration and other activities. Staff speaks Euskara and Spanish.

Delegación en Baleares. Oversees mountaineering activities in Spain's Balearic Islands in the Mediterranean off the Costa del Azahar. Affiliated with 12 local clubs devoted to mountaineering and cave exploration. Staff speaks Catalan and Spanish.

Maps

The *Mapa Topográfico Nacional de España,* in a scale of 1:50,000, covers all of Spain, including the Canary Islands and Balearic Islands. Peninsular Spain is covered by 1,620 sheets. They show many—but not all—country tracks, bridle paths and footpaths, in addition to towns, roads, vegetation and other land and water features. Relief is indicated by both shading and contour lines. When using these sheets, be sure to check the survey dates, which range from the 1970s back to the turn of the century. Because older maps sometimes contain serious inaccuracies, you should consult local residents in order to verify existing footpaths or other features subject to change.

A few areas are also covered by 1:25,000 sheets. As yet, however, the 1:25,000 series, entitled the *Mapa Topográfico Nacional,* is far from complete and no index to existing sheets is available. Few exist for Spain's mountain regions.

Both map series, as well as an index to the 1:50,000 sheets and a catalog of publications are available from:

Instituto Geográfico Nacional (see *Address Directory*).

When ordering maps, be sure to specify which series you want and the appropriate sheet numbers. Correspondence should be in Spanish.

The I.G.N. topographical maps are also available from:

Llibreria Quera (see Address Directory). The best bookstore in Spain for walkers. Specializes in books and maps on walking, climbing, skiing, cave exploration and natural history. Stocks an exhaustive inventory of maps and guides. Excellent mail-order service. Letters addressed to the bookstore may be written in Spanish, French or English; replies are in Spanish only. Walkers from all parts of Spain order maps and guides from this store. There is no better place in Spain to obtain these materials.

Regional Maps & Map-Guides

Spain's principal walking areas are covered by a variety of topographical maps, sketch maps and map-guides designed with the walker in mind. Some are published by the F.E.M., some by local walking clubs and some by private publishers. All are available from the Llibreria Quera. Local walking clubs often carry a small supply of those covering their regions. The F.E.M. office in Madrid can supply any of the maps and map-guides it publishes, as well as those covering the Sierra de Gredos and Sierra de Guadarrama.

The term *mapa-guía* (map-guide) is used in Spain to designate: 1) walking guides that include topographical maps or sketch maps *(mapas croquises)* showing footpaths and other walking routes, and 2) special walking maps with or without descriptive texts.

Map-guides that include a booklet or brochure with separate text are described in the following section on guidebooks. Those that are essentially walking maps are listed below.

One of the most extensive series of walking maps published in Spain is the *Mapas-Guías de Macizos Montañosos Españoles*. Each sheet covers a particular mountain massif in the Cordillera Cantábrica, the Pyrenees or the Sistema Ibérico. The maps come in various scales and show both footpaths and refuges. In addition, each sheet lists suggested walks and walking times, and includes sketches of mountain panoramas and other information. All are available from Llibreria Quera.

Walking maps available to the principal mountain regions of Spain include the following:

Cordillera Cantábrica & the Picos de Europa

- *Macizo Central de Picos de Europa,* 1:22,000 (in Spanish), by J. M. Boada, 1935. A topographical map showing walking routes in the central massif of the Picos de Europa.

- *Picos de Europa,* 1:100,000 (in Spanish), by José Arias Corcho, 1972. A color-shaded relief sketch map showing walking routes, jeep tracks and roads. Lists eight refuges. The back of the map has eight line drawings of panoramic vistas in the range; descriptions of geography, flora and fauna; information on highways and railroads providing access to the range; and a list of driving itineraries.

- *Mapas-Guías de Macizos Montañosos Españoles* (in Spanish). Includes the following 28 map sheets:
  —A-10 *Cuenca Alta del Rio Luna,* 1:50,000, including Picos Albos, Cañada and Cirbanal.
  —A-12 *Lagos de Saliencia,* 1:50,000, including Llagüenzos.
  —A-14 *Puerto Ventana,* 1:35,000, including Peña Ubiña.
  —A-16 *Puerto de Pajares,* 1:50,000, including Cellón-Brañacaballo.

—A-18 *Puerto de San Isidro,* 1:50,000, including Puerto Huevo, Nogales, Torres and Peñas Agujas.

—A-20 *Puertos del Ponton y la Tarna,* 1:50,000, from Mampodre to Gildar.

—A-22 *Montes de Riaño,* 1:35,000, including Llordas, Pas. Pintas, Neredo and Cerroso.

—A-32 *Picos de Europa,* 1:30,000, covering the Macizos de Urrieles (Central) and de Andara (Occidental).

—A-40 *Alto Carrion,* 1:50,000.

—A-41 *Alto Luriana,* 1:50,000, including Peña Pireta.

—A-44 *Alto Campoo y Peña Sagra,* 1:50,000.

The following sheets cover the Montes Vascos:

—B-3 *Vega de Pas, Soba, Valdeporres, Espinosa de los Monteros,* 1:50,000.

—B-5 *Soba, Ruesga, Ampuero y Encartaciones,* 1:50,000.

—B-7 *Montes de Ordunte—Sierras Magdalena y Burdieta,* 1:50,000.

—B-9 *Tobalina y Valdegobia,* 1:50,000.

—B-11 *De Valdegobia a Losa,* 1:50,000.

—B-13 *Encartaciones,* 1:40,000, covering the Zona Central.

—B-14 *Encartaciones,* 1:30,000, covering the Zona Oriental.

—B-15 *Macizo de Ganekogorta,* 1:35,000.

—B-17 *Macizo de Gorbea,* 1:35,000.

—B-19 *Aramotz y Eskubaratz,* 1:35,000.

—B-20 *Duranguesado y Aranguio,* 1:35,000.

—B-21 *Cuenca alta del Deva,* 1:35,000.

—B-23 *Sierras de Alona—Aizkorri—Elguea—Urkilla—Altzania,* 1:35,000.

—B-24 *Sierra de Altzania,* 1:35,000.

—B-25 *Macizo de Aralar,* 1:35,000.

—B-26 *Urbasa y Andia,* 1:50,000.

—B-27 *Cantabria,* 1:50,000, from Toloño to Codés.

• *Peña Ubiña,* 1:50,000 (in Spanish), by J. R. Lueje and José Antonio Odriozola, F.E.M., 1975. Topographical map.

• *Tres Macizos de los Picos de Europa,* 1:50,000 (in Spanish), by Jose Antonio Odriozola, F.E.M., 1975. Topographical map.

• *Tres Macizos de los Picos de Europa,* 1:50,000 (in Spanish), by Juan Llop, Federación Asturiana de Montañismo. Topographical map showing walking routes and the locations of existing mountain refuges. Also includes a general refuge plan showing those now under construction and planned for the future.

The Pyrenees

- *Aigua de Valls—Llinars de l'Aiguadora—Capolat*, 1:25,000, Club Excursionista Pirenaic, 1974. Sketch map showing footpaths, with information on history and geography of the Pyrenees.
- *Llinars de l'Aigua d'Ora—Serra de Peguera*, 1:25,000, Federación Catalana de Montañismo and Club Excursionista Pirenaic, 1974. Topographical map showing roads, tracks, footpaths and refuges.
- *Mapa-Guías de Macizos Montañosos Españoles* (in Spanish). Includes the following six map sheets:
  —C-3 *Valle de Belagua*, 1:40,000.
  —C-4 *Valles de Anso y Hecho*, 1:35,000.
  —C-7 *Circo de Piedrafita, Panticosa*, 1:35,000.
  —C-8 *Del Aragon al Gallego*, 1:50,000, including Collarada, Escarra and Telera.
  —C-9 *Sierra de Tendeñera*, 1:50,000.
  —C-10 *Goriz*, 1:40,000.
- *Pirineo Central*, 1:50,000 (in Spanish), by R. Cebrian. Sketch map.
- *Pirineo Central*, 1:80,000 (in Spanish), by R. Cebrian. Sketch map in four sheets: *Ansabere, Balaitus, Mone Perdido* and *Posets*.

The Sistema Central

- *Pedriza de Manzanares*, 1:10,000 (in Spanish), F.E.M., 1967. Sketch map of an important massif in the Sierra de Guadarrama, with a panoramic drawing, description of the massif and information on its geology and ecology.
- *Sierra de Gredos*, 1:50,000 (in Spanish), F.E.M., 1977. Sketch map with a panoramic drawing.
- *Sierra de Guadarrama*, 1:50,000 (in Spanish), F.E.M. and the Instituto Geográfico Nacional, 1973. Topographical map consisting of I.G.N. Mapa Topográfico Nacional, sheets 483, 484, 508 and 509.
- *Sistema Central*, 1:50,000 (in Spanish), by J. A. Fenollera, Federación Castellana de Montañismo, 1971-1973. Sketch map in eight sheets of the Sierra de Guadarrama, Sierra de Gredos and subordinate ranges.

Sistema Ibérico

- *Mapas-Guías de Macizos Montañosos Españoles* (in Spanish). Includes the following seven map sheets:

—D-1 *Sierras de Mencilla y la Demanda*, 1:50,000.
—D-2 *Sierra de la Demanda*, 1:50,000.
—D-3 *Urbion y Campiña*, 1:60,000.
—D-4 *Sierra Cebollera*, 1:60,000.
—D-5 *Camero Nuevo*, 1:50,000.
—D-7 *Moncayo*, 1:50,000.
—D-9 *Sierra de Javalambre—Sierra de Gudar*, 1:50,000.

Sistema Penibético & the Sierra Nevada

- *Sierra Nevada, Sector Occidental*, 1:50,000 (in Spanish), Editorial Montblanc, Granollers, 1965. Topographical map of the western Sierra Nevada, showing roads, tracks and footpaths in red. A companion to the *Guía de Sierra Nevada* (see section on Guidebooks).
- *Sierra Nevada*, 1:50,000 (in Spanish), Federación Andaluza de Montañismo.
- *Sierra Nevada*, 1:50,000 (in Spanish), F.E.M. In preparation.

Guidebooks

There are more than 100 guidebooks to walking in Spain, but the coverage is very uneven. For example, while the Pyrenees have been the subject of numerous walking and climbing guides (including some published in France), there is only one guide each for the Sierra Nevada, Picos de Europa and Sierra de Guadarrama and none for the Sierra de Gredos, Sistema Ibérico and many other important walking regions. Moreover, some of the guides are sketchy, providing maps and route summaries, but little or nothing in the way of detailed descriptions of possible walks.

There is only one walking guide that covers Spain as a whole:

- *Bergwelt Spaniens* (in German) by Agustin Jolis, Fink-Kümmerly + Frey, Stuttgart, 1973. Describes 115 day hikes in Catalunya, the Pyrenees, the Cordillera Cantábrica, the Sistema Central and the Sierra Nevada. Available from GEO Center, Internationales Landkartenhaus, Stuttgart, Germany (see *Address Directory*).

The Guía-Cartográfica series published by Editorial Alpina consists of slim guidebooks accompanied by special topographical maps on which walking routes are shown in red. These guides are very useful for the regions they cover: Catalunya, the Picos de Europa, the Pyrenees and the Sierra de Guadarrama. The text describes the geography, geology, climate and vegetation of the region covered; available lodgings, mountain refuges and transportation; and suggested walking and climbing excursions. Thus far, there are more than 55 titles in the series, including 16 ski mountaineering guides, and new ones are published regularly. Individual titles are listed below under the appropriate mountain regions. The series is published by:

Editorial Alpina (see *Address Directory*).

All titles in the series are available from Llibreria Quera. Several of the local walking clubs publish a series of leaflets, generally known as *fichas*, each of which describes one or two walking routes and includes a sketch map. These are often only available from the club that publishes them. A few of the *fichas* series are listed below. Information on those covering other mountain areas can be obtained from the regional or provincial mountaineering federation for the area in which you intend to walk.

Where walking guides do not exist, you can plan your own itineraries by using the appropriate maps and map-guides in conjunction with the tourist brochures and general guidebooks available to most of Spain's principal walking regions. The following regional list includes walking guides, climbing guides and tourist guides, some of which include descriptions of suggested walks.

Catalunya

Walking Guides

Available from Llibreria Quera (see *Address Directory)*:

- *Berguedà i Lluçanes* (in Catalan) by J. Sala i Sivillà, Colecció Arxiu Bibliogràfic de la Unió Excursionista de Catalunya, Barcelona. A 503-page guide commemorating a century of walking in Catalunya. Includes photographs, drawings and topographical maps.
- *Camins i Canals de Montserrat: Guía d'Inineraris* (in Catalan) by Ramon Ribera, Colecció Cavall Bernat. Describes 58 walking routes in the mountain sectors of Monistrol, Monestir de Montserrat, Santa Cecilia, Collbató and El Bruc. Includes a topographical map in a scale of 1:75,000.
- *Guías-Cartográficas* (in Catalan and Spanish), Editorial Alpina, Granollers. Includes the following 16 titles:
  —*Cingles de Bertí y de Gallifa*, 1:25,000.
  —*El Corredor—Mataró*, 1:25,000.
  —*Costa Brava I: Tossa*, 1:25,000.
  —*Costa Brava II: Cadaqués*, 1:80,000.
  —*El Farell—Granollers—Sabadell*, 1:25,000.
  —*Garraf—Castelldefels*, 1:25,000.

—*Gran Barcelona*, 1:25,000.
—*Les Guilleries—Collsacabra*, 1:40,000.
—*Moianès*, 1:25,000.
—*Montnegre—Hortsavinyà*, 1:25,000.
—*El Montseny*, 1:40,000.
—*Montserrat*, 1:10,000 and 1:40,000.
—*Ordal*, 1:25,000.
—*St. Lorenç del Munt y Serra de l'Obac*, 1:25,000.
—*Sant Mateu—Cercanías de Barcelona*, 1:25,000.
—*S. Salvador de les Espases—Terrassa*, 1:25,000.

* *Topo-Guia G.R. 7* (in Spanish and Catalan) by the Federació d'Entitats Excursionistes de Catalunya, Editorial SERPA, Barcelona. Describes the portion of long-distance footpath GR-7 from the Andorran frontier through Catalunya to Fredes, in Valencia. In seven volumes: 1) *de la Seu d'Urgell al Santuari del Miracle*, 2) *del Santuari del Miracle a Belpratt*, 3) *de Belpratt a la Riba*, 4) *de la Riba al Coll de la Teixeta*, 5) *dell Coll de la Teixeta a Tivissa*, 6) *de Tivissa a Paüls*, 7) *de Paüls a Fredes*. The guidebooks can be used to walk in either direction; descriptions are written in Catalan for one direction, in Spanish for the other. The guidebooks include maps, route profiles to show elevation differences—and the steepness of climbs and descents—plus the distances and walking times between points enroute. Format is similar to that of the French topo-guides.

* *Cerdanya* (in Spanish) by Agustí Jolis and M.ª Antònia Simó de Jolis, Colección de Guias del Centre Excursionista de Catalunya, Club Alpí Català, Editorial Montblanc, Barcelona. An extremely good guide to walks, climbs, ski tours and winter ascents in the Pyrenees in and around Andorra. Includes details on geography, geology, flora, fauna, climate and mountain refuges. Illustrated with numerous line drawings and sketch maps. (Recommended)

* *Alt Berguedà i Cardener* (in Spanish). A companion guide to *Cerdanya* by the same authors and from the same series. Covers the mountain region south of Andorra, stretching from Seu d'Urgell to Solsona and including the ranges above the town of Berga. (Recommended)

* *Pedraforca* (in Spanish). Also from the Colección de Guias del Centre Excursionista de Catalunya. Excerpted from Chapter VII of *Alt Berguedà i Cardener*.

Available from Arxiu Bibliogràfic de la Unió Excursionista de Catalunya (see *Address Directory):*

* *Itineraris pel Berguedà, Ripolles i Garrotxa* (in Catalan) by J.R. and B.C.
* *Ermites del Vallès* (in Catalan) by J. Serra Roselló.
* *Itineraris pel Vallès Occidental i Baix Llobregat* (in Catalan) by David M. Aloy and M. Mercè Lleonart.

- *Excursió a les Cartoixes de Catalunya* (in Catalan) by Bernat del Gaìa.
- *Itineraris a Castells i Breus Notíces Històriques* (in Catalan) by Salvador Miralda.
- *El Camí ral d'Aragó* (in Catalan) by Ramon Morales.
- *Separates "Senderos" i "Excursionisme"* (in Catalan). A series of 19 *fichas*, each describing one or two walks. Availability varies. A list of titles currently in stock can be obtained from the Arxiu Bibliogràfic de la Unió Excursionista de Catalunya.

The Unió Excursionista de Catalunya publishes several other titles, including books on camping, climbing, and the maps covering Catalunya. A complete list of titles is available on request. You may write in Catalan, Spanish or French.

Climbing Guides

Available from Llibreria Quera:

- *Roques, Parets i Agulles de Montserrat: 3/Regió de Tabor* (in Catalan) by J. M. Rodés and F. Labraña, Colecció Cavall Bernat. Describes climbs in the mountains of the Tabor region, near Montserrat.

Tourist Guides

Available from Llibreria Quera:

- *Guía de Catalunya* (in Catalan) by Josep M. Armengou. Includes descriptions of automobile, tourist and walking itineraries.
- *Guías Turisticas Everest* (in Spanish), Editorial Everest, León. Several titles covering various areas in Catalunya, including the Costa Brava and the provinces of Barcelona and Gerona. A complete list of titles can be obtained from Llibreria Quera.

The Cordillera Cantábrica & Picos de Europa

Walking Guides

Available from Llibreria Quera:

- *Picos de Europa* (in Spanish), Editorial Alpina, Granollers. Two Guías-Cartográficas: 1) *I: Macizo Occidental* and 2) *II: Naranjo de Bulnes, Macizos Central y Oriental*. Includes descriptions of walks and 1:25,000 topographical maps with routes shown in red.

Climbing Guides

Available from the Federación Palentina de Montañismo:

- *Fuentes Carrionas* (in Spanish) by the Federación Palentina de Montañismo, Palencia, 1973. A brochure describing the peaks and valleys at the headwaters of the Río Carrion, in the province of Palencia. The emphasis is on climbing routes, but the brochure also contains information of use to the walker. Includes photographic panoramas of the peaks, each labeled with their name, climbing routes and records; a list of notable peaks and their elevations; a description of snow conditions and skiing routes; a list of towns and villages; information on geology and flora and fauna; a general description of the area; information on cave exploration; and a sketch map of the region showing roads, rough tracks, ski routes and footpaths.
- *Guía del Macizo del Alto Carrion* (in Spanish) by the Federación Palentina de Montañismo, Palencia, 1978. A booklet describing climbing routes in the Alto Carrion. Includes two sketch maps showing footpaths. Climbing routes are shown on drawings and photographs of the peaks.

Tourist Guides

Available as noted below:

- *De Peña Labra a las Tuerces* (in Spanish) by the Federación Palentina de Montañismo, Palencia, 1967. A brochure providing general information on the Sierra de Peña Labra, in Palencia province. Includes a general description of the region and information on geology, cave exploration, flora and fauna and local towns and villages. A sketch map shows roads, tracks and footpaths. Available from the Federación Palentina de Montañismo.
- *Los Picos de Europa* (in Spanish) by José Ramon Lueje, Editorial Everest, León. Provides general tourist information for the Picos de Europa. Available from Llibreria Quera.
- *Picos de Europa* (in English), Secretaria de Estado del Turismo, Madrid. Provides general information on the Picos de Europa. Includes a color-shaded relief map showing some footpaths and has numerous color photographs. Available from local tourist information offices (see list of addresses under, *Oficina Information de Turismo,in the* **Address Directory).**

Montañas Gallegas & the Sierra y Picos de Ancares

Walking Guides

Available from the Club Montañeros Celtas:

- *Cumbres de Galicia: Monte Alba* (in Spanish) by the Club Montañeros Celtas, Vigo, 1976. The first in a series of guides to be published on the mountains of Galicia.

Tourist Guides

Available from the Oficina de Información y Turismo, Lugo:

- *Sierra de Ancares* (in English), Secretaria de Estado del Turismo, Madrid. Provides general information on the Sierra y Picos de Ancares. Includes a color-shaded relief map and numerous color photographs.

The Pyrenees

Walking Guides

Available from Llibreria Quera:

- *A la Découverte de la Sierra de Guara* (in French) by Pierre Minivielle, Editions Marrimpouey Jeune, Pau, France, 1974. Describes 100 walks in the spectacular canyonlands of the Sierra de Guara, a foothill range south of the central Pyrenees. Each walk is described in detail and is shown in red on sketch maps. Walking times are included with the route descriptions. Also includes information on the geology, geography, wildlife, history and culture of the Sierra de Guara, as well as on transportation, food and lodgings, equipment and safety. Illustrated with photographs, sketch maps and line drawings.

- *Colección de Guías del Centre Escursionista de Catalunya, Club Alpí Català* (in Spanish). Editorial Montblanc, Barcelona. A series of 10 guides to the walks, climbs and auto routes in the Pyrenees of Aragon and Catalunya. Exhaustive coverage of each region includes dozens—even hundreds—of route descriptions, as well as information on geography, geology, climate, flora, fauna and mountain refuges. Includes cross-country ski routes and winter ascents. Each walk description not only gives the walking time required for the entire route, but indicates the times it takes to get from one point to the next along the way. Climbing routes are rated according to difficulty and are shown on excellent line-drawings of the various massifs. Sketch maps showing walking routes are included with each volume. The volumes in the series are: 1) *Vignemale-Monte Perdido* by Robert Ollivier, 1st edition, 1968; 2) *Posets-Maladeta* (in French) by André Armengaud and Agustí Jolis, 3rd edition, 1968; 3) *Pallars-Aran* by Agustí Jolis and M.ª Antònia Simó de Jolis, 4th edition, 1971; 4) *Urgellet-Pica d'Estats* by Agustí Jolis and M.ª Antònia Simó de Jolis; 5) *Alt Berguedà i Cardener* by Agustí Jolis and M.ª Antònia Simó de Jolis, 3rd edition, 1965; 6) *Pedraforca* (constitutes Chapter VII of the guide *Alt Berguedà i Cardener);* 7) *Cerdanya* (including Andorra) by Agustí Jolis and M.ª Antònia Simó de Jolis, 3rd edition, 1969; and 8) *Rosselló* by Agustí Jolis and M.ª Antònia Simó de Jolis. Highly recommended.

• *Guías-Cartográficas* (in Spanish), Editorial Alpina, Granollers. Includes the following 23 titles:
—*Andorra i Sectors Fronterers,* 1:40,000.
—*Bachimala—Cotiella,* 1:25,000 and 1:40,000.
—*Costabona—Coll d'Ares,* 1:25,000.
—*Garrotxa—Comanegra—Bassegoda—El Mont—Olot—Banyoles,* 1:40,000.
—*La Maladeta—Aneto,* 1:25,000.
—*Montardo—Aigües Tortes,* 1:25,000.
—*Montgrony—Fonts de Llobregat,* 1:25,000.
—*Montsec,* 1:25,000.
—*Montsent de Pallars—Llessui,* 1:25,000.
—*Moixeró—La Molina,* 1:25,000.
—*Ordesa—Vignemale,*1:40,000.
—*Pica d'Estats—Montroig—Ribera de Cardós,* 1:25,000.
—*Pont de Suert—Escales,* 1:25,000.
—*Port del Comte—Serra del Verd,* 1:25,000.
—*Posets—Benasque,* 1:25,000.
—*Puigmal—Núria,* 1:25,000.
—*Puigsacalm—Bellmunt,* 1:25,000.
—*Rasos de Peguera—Serra d'Ensija,* 1:25,000.
—*La Ribagorca,* 1:25,000.
—*Sant Maurici—Els Encantats,* 1:25,000.
—*Serra del Cadí y Pedraforca,* 1:25,000.
—*Taga—Valls de Ribes i S. Joan,* 1:25,000.
—*La Vall d'Aran,* 1:40,000.

• *Haute Randonnée Pyrénéenne* (in French) by Georges Veron, Club Alpin Français, Paris, 2nd ed., 1976. Describes 45 walks, plus alternate routes, in the entire Pyrenees. Includes 53 1:50,000 topographical maps and seven other maps. The only walking guide covering the entire range.

• *Rutas Montañeras* (in Spanish) by the Club Deportivo Navarra, Diario de Navarra, Pamplona, 1973. In two volumes: 1) *I: Roncal-Zuria* and 2) *II: Ory-Velate.* The two books describe dozens of walks in the Pyrenees of Navarre. Routes are shown on separate sketch maps accompanying each volume. Route descriptions include walking times between points along the way.

• *Pyrénées Centrales* (in French), Editions Robert Ollivier, Pau, France. In three volumes: 1) *Vol. I: Cauterets—Vignemale—Gavernie—Cañons Espagnols* by D. Minvielle, R. Ollivier and J. and P. Ravier, 1965; describes 318 walking and climbing routes; includes numerous illustrations and sketch maps; 2) *Vol. II: Bigorre—*

Arbizon—Neouvielle—Troumouse by X. Defos du Rau, R. Ollivier and J. and P. Ravier, 1968; describes over 300 walking and climbing routes; numerous illustrations and sketch maps; and 3) in the French Pyrenees: *Vol. III: Vallées d'Aure et de Luchon* by A. Armengaud, F. Cormet, R. Ollivier and J. and P. Ravier, 1969.

- *Pyrénées Occidentales* (in French), Editions Robert Ollivier, Pau, France. In two volumes: 1) *Vol. I: Aspe et Ossau* by G. Boisson, R. Ollivier and J. and P. Ravier, 1960; describes 255 walking routes and climbs; numerous illustrations and sketch maps; 2) *Vol. II: De la vallée d'Ossau au val d'Azun* by G. Boisson, R. Ollivier and J. and P. Ravier, 1963; describes 357 walking routes and climbs; numerous illustrations and sketch maps.

Available from West Col Productions:

- *Pyrenees West* (in English) by Battagel. Covers Lescun, Aspe, Ossau, Eaux-Bonnes, Balaitous, Marcadau, Vignemale, Gavarnie, Perdido and Añisclo.
- *Pyrenees East* (in English) by Battagel. Covers all main groups east of Gavarnie cirque including Maladeta and the Spanish national parks.
- *Pyrenees High Level Route* (in French) by Georges Veron. See description for *Haute Randonnée Pyrenéenne* under the listing of guidebooks available from Llibreria Quera.

Other guidebooks covering the French Pyrenees are listed in *On Foot Through Europe: A Trail Guide to France & the Benelux Nations.*

Ski Touring & Ski Mountaineering Guides

Available from Llibreria Quera:

- *Fixtes Esquí* (in Catalan, Spanish and French) by Enric Font, Xavier Gregori and Joseph M. Sala of the Centre Excursionista de Catalunya, Editorial Alpina, Granollers. A series of guides describing ski touring routes, climbs and traverses in the Pyrenees. Each route is fully described and includes a sketch map, information on its difficulty, skiing time and a list of the required topographical maps. The geography of each region is also briefly described. The series includes the following titles:
  —*Travessía dels Tres Colls* (Núria)
  —*Tuc de Baciver* (Vall d'Aran)
  —*Tuc d'era Pincela* (Vall d'Aran)
  —*Tuc d'era Salana* (Vall d'Aran)
  —*P. Subenuix–P. Morto* (Pallars)
  —*Pic de la Serrera* (Andorra)
  —*Pic de la Coma Pedrosa* (Andorra)

—*Montardo* (Alta Ribagorça)
—*Vallibierna* (Alta Ribagorça)
—*Tuc de Mulleres* (Alta Ribagorça-Vall d'Aran)
—*Pic de Norís* (Pallars)
—*Mont-Roig* (Pallars)
—*Balaitús* (from Glera to Neus)
—*Posets* (via Viadós)
—*Pic de Bassiero Est* (Pallars)
—*Pic de Certascan Nord* (Pallars)
Sixteen other titles are in preparation.

Climbing Guides

Available from Llibreria Quera:

- *Los Pirineos: Las 100 Mejores Ascensiones y Excursiones* (in Spanish) by Partice de Bellefon, Editorial RM. Describes approaches, climbing routes and descent routes in each of the major ranges of the Pyrenees Cordillera.
- *Pics de mès de 2.000 Metres al Pirineu Català, Sector Oriental* (in Catalan) by Josep Llaudó i Majoral, Colecció Arxiu Bibliogràfic Excursionista de la Unió Excursionista de Catalunya, Barcelona.
- Also see the volumes in the *Colección de Guías del Centre Excursionista de Catalunya, Pyrénées Centrales* and *Pyrénées Occidentales* series listed above.

Tourist Guides

Available from Llibreria Quera, except where noted otherwise:

- *El Parque Nacional de Aigues Tortes y Lago de San Mauricio* (in Spanish) by C. Carrasco-Munoz, Editorial Everest, León.
- *El Pirineo Aragones* (in Spanish) by S. Broto, Editorial Everest, León.
- *El Pirineo Catalan* (in Spanish), Editorial Everest, León.
- *El Pirineo Navarro* (in Spanish) by Jaime del Burgo, Editorial Everest, León.
- *Por el Pirineo Aragones (Rutas de la Jacetania)* (in Spanish) by Cayetano Enriquez de Salamanca, Madrid.
- *Por el Pirineo Aragones (Rutas del Sobrarbe y la Rigagorza* (in Spanish) by Cayetano Enriquez de Salamanca, Madrid.
- *Por el Pirineo Catalan I: Valle de Arán y Parque Nacional de Aigües Tortes* (in Spanish) by Cayetano Enriquez de Salamanca, Madrid.
- *Por el Pirineo Catalan II: El Pallars, El Alto Urgel y Andorra* (in Spanish) by Cayetano Enriquez de Salamanca, Madrid.

- *Por el Pirineo Catalan III: Cerdanya, Alto Berguedà y Ripollés* (in Spanish) by Cayetano Enriquez de Salamanca, Madrid.
- *The Pyrenees, Spain* (in English), Secretaria de Estado del Turismo, Madrid. Tourist brochure available free of charge from local tourist offices (see *Address Directory*).

Sistema Central

Walking Guides

Available from Llibreria Quera:

- *Guadarrama* (in Spanish), Editorial Alpina, Granollers. Includes suggested walks and a 1:25,000 topographical map with routes shown in red.

Tourist Guides

Available as noted below:

- *Gredos, por Dentro y por Fuera* (in Spanish) by Cayetano Enriquez de Salamanca. Available from Llibreria Quera.
- *Sierra de Gredos* (in English), Secretaria de Estado del Turismo, Madrid. Tourist brochure with brief summaries of seven walking routes. Available free of charge from local tourist offices.
- *Sierra de Guadarrama* (in English), Secretaria de Estado del Turismo, Madrid. Brochure available free of charge from local tourist offices.

Sistema Penibético & the Sierra Nevada

Walking Guides

Available as noted below:

- *Guía de Sierra Nevada* (in Spanish) by P. Bueno, Editorial Montblanc, Granollers. A companion to the 1:50,000 topographical map, *Sierra Nevada, Sector Occidental* (see section on Maps). Available from Llibreria Quera.
- *Itinerarios del Macizo de Sierra Nevada* (in Spanish), by Antonio Castillo Rodrígues and Aurelio del Castillo Amaro, published by a variety of local mountaineering clubs and sport shops. In two series: 1) *Recorridos de Baja Montaña* and 2) *Recorridos de Alta Montaña*. Each series consists of a series of leaflets *(fichas)* describing walks in the Sierra Nevada. Each leaflet describes one or two routes, gives walking times, indicates the difficulty of the route or routes, describes conditions in winter and includes a sketch map showing the route, plus peaks, lakes, streams and refuges along the way.

Available from walking clubs, book stores and sport shops in Granada.

- *Las Montañas de Alicante* (in Spanish) by Antonio Callero Pico, Colección CP. Describes excursions in the sierras of Alicante province. Available from Libreria Esteban Sanz and Llibreria Quera.
- *Sierra Nevada* (in English) by Manuel Ferrer, Editorial Anel, Granada. An extensive general guide to the range. Includes suggested walks. Available from Llibreria Quera.

Climbing Guides

- *Vias de Escalada de Sierra Nevada* (in Spanish), Federación Andaluza de Montañismo.

Tourist Guides

- *Sierra de Cazorla* (in English), Secretaria de Estado del Turismo, Madrid. Brochure available free of charge from local tourist offices.
- *Sierra Nevada* (in Spanish), Editorial Everest, León.
- *Sierra Nevada* (in English), Secretaria de Estado del Turismo, Madrid. Brochure available free of charge from local tourist offices.

Other guidebooks may be available to Spain's various mountain ranges. For a list of titles, write to Llibreria Quera, specify the mountain area in which you are interested and ask for one of its catalogs.

Trailside Lodgings

A wide variety of lodgings is available to walkers in Spain. There are lavish, state-owned *paradores* (tourist hotels) and *albergues* (wayside inns), many situated in the mountains; private hotels and inns; youth hostels; and mountain huts, most owned by the local walking clubs. In addition, you can usually find shelter in a Forest Service lean-to, a shepherd's hut or an old, abandoned chapel tucked away in the hills.

Private accommodation in *posadas* (inns), *fondas* and *pensions* (guesthouses) and *hostales* (inexpensive hotels) is available in most of the larger mountain towns. In the smaller villages, which often lack public accommodation, you can generally find a covered spot to sleep by simply asking the mayor for assistance.

Hotel rates are much lower in Spain than in most other countries in Europe. And the pensions and hostels are very inexpensive. The prices for all public lodgings are approved by the government and posted in an obvious place in each room. There are stiff penalties for overcharging. Blue signs posted on the outside of the buildings indicate what sort of lodging it is—*H:* hotel; *H* with an *S* in it: hostal; and *R:* residencia or guesthouse.

A list of privately owned hotels, inns and guesthouses is available on request from the Secretaria de Estado del Turismo (see *Address Directory*).

Mountain Refuges

Mountain refuges are found in valleys, and on mountain slopes, passes and ridges in all of Spain's principal mountain ranges. These refuges are basically of three types: 1) *paradores*, 2) *albergues* and 3) mountain huts.

The *paradores* are state-owned tourist hotels offering a full range of services, including restaurants, lounges, private baths, hot and cold running water, central heating, a telephone in each room and so on. Many are located in remodeled castles or other historic buildings.

The *albergues* may be either state- or privately owned. They offer comfortable accommodation on a somewhat more modest scale than the *paradores*. Some are housed in fine old buildings, however, and a few even have swimming pools. All serve meals. *Paradores* and *albergues* alike are situated on public highways.

A color brochure entitled *Paradores y Albergues: Spain,* listing state-owned *paradores* and *albergues* and including a map of Spain showing their locations, is available from the Secretaria de Estado del Turismo.

For simpler accommodation there are numerous mountain huts scattered throughout the Pyrenees, Cordillera Cantábrica, Sierra Nevada, Sierra de Guadarrama, Sierra de Gredos and other ranges. All but a few of these huts are owned by Spain's various mountaineering clubs. Most are unattended because they do not receive enough use to merit guardians.

Facilities at most huts are spartan by Alpine standards. If you plan to use the huts, be sure to carry your own food, stove, cooking kit and sleeping bag. You should also plan to do a little cleaning up since unattended huts are inevitably left dirty.

In order to use the huts you must be a member of one of the walking clubs affiliated with the F.E.M. or of one of the foreign clubs with which the F.E.M. has exchange privileges. Most of the huts are kept locked, so you must obtain a key from the local club that owns the hut. Wherever possible, it is best to make arrangements for picking up the necessary keys before you arrive in Spain.

The best way to find out where the huts in any given region are located—and who owns them—is to write the local walking clubs and request information on their particular huts, if any. Many issue leaflets describing their huts and, in some cases, listing suggested walks in the vicinity of each. The addresses of local clubs are given in the *F.E.M. Annuario* (see description under the section on Spain's Walking Clubs). Or you can obtain them from the regional or provincial mountaineering federation with which they are affiliated (see *Address Directory*).

The Secretaria de Estado del Turismo publishes an excellent and beautiful set of guidebooks to the mountain refuges in Spain:

- *Guia: Refugios de Montaña.* In 3 volumes: 1) *Tomo I: Pireneos;* 2)

Tomo II: Sistema Ibérico y Sistema Central; and 3) Tomo III: Cordillera Cantábrica, Picos de Europa, Montañas Galacias (in Spanish). Each volume is lavishly illustrated with color photographs of the various mountain ranges and worth owning for this reason alone. There is also a color photograph of each refuge and a sketch map showing its location as well as nearby roads, footpaths and topographical features. For each hut, the guides list its name, owner, location, capacity, access, altitude, nearby peaks and rivers, dates of operation and available facilities. Available from Llibreria Quera Recommended.

Youth Hostels

Spain has 69 youth hostels spread throughout the country. Some accommodate men only; and some, women only. Most of the hostels are open only during the summer. Further information is available from:

Red Española de Albergues Juveniles (Spanish Youth Hostel Association). See *Address Directory*. Open Monday through Friday, 9 a.m. to 2 p.m.

Camping

If you plan extended walks in the mountains of Spain, you should be prepared to camp. Although there are many mountain refuges, they are scattered among numerous ranges and may be few and far between in any given area. The refuge network is densest in the Pyrenees and Picos de Europa. In other mountain regions there may be only one or two refuges—if any—serving a large area.

Camping is permitted on all public lands in Spain, except: 1) within one kilometer of towns, 2) within 50 meters of a main road, 3) within 150 meters of waters flowing into reservoirs, 4) in the vicinity of historic buildings, 5) in places prohibited by local authorities, 6) in regions reserved for fishing and hunting, and 7) in forestry areas except where prior permission has been obtained from the Servicio Forestal. Camping on private lands is forbidden without the express permission of the owner. In addition, fires are prohibited within 200 meters of any forest. Failure to observe these restrictions will likely bring a midnight visit from the Guardia Civil.

Spain has nearly 200 public campgrounds, the majority of which are located near the coasts. A map entitled Mapa de Campings España showing their locations and listing their facilities is available from the Secretaria de Estado del Turismo.

Water

The water in mountain streams is generally safe to drink except below sheep pastures or habitations. Water is plentiful in the Pyrenees, Sierra de Guadarrama and mountains of Catalunya, Galicia and Valencia. It is scarce, however, in the Picos de Europa and Sierra Nevada, where you should be prepared to carry your own.

City tap water is safe to drink, although heavily chlorinated. In the country, you should make sure a water source is safe before drinking. Bad water is supposed to be marked *no potable,* but it might be a good idea to inquire locally in any case. During the summer, there is an occasional danger of typhoid from contaminated rural water sources.

Equipment Notes

The equipment necessary for walking in the mountains of Spain is the same as that for most high mountain ranges in Europe. In addition, typical conditions in Spain make it advisable to carry the following items:

1. Sun hat and salt tablets. Spanish summers are very hot, and the sun is especially intense at high altitudes. Special care should be taken to prevent sunstroke and heat exhaustion.

2. Be sure to carry your own water when walking in the Sierra Nevada or Picos de Europa.

3. If you plan to use the mountain huts, carry your own food, stove, cooking kit and sleeping bag.

Walking Tours & Mountain Guides

Most of the local walking clubs in Spain conduct walking and climbing tours for their members. A calendar of these tours and other activities organized by the local clubs may be obtained from the provincial and regional mountaineering federations to which the clubs are affiliated. All arrangements for participating in the tours, however, must be made directly with the sponsoring club before your arrival in the country. Any F.E.M. member or member of the alpine and mountaineering clubs with which the F.E.M. is affiliated in Europe is eligible to participate in tours conducted by the club. If you are not a club member, you must either plan your own walks or, for climbs, hire a mountain guide.

Although the system of mountain guides is not as well developed as in the Alpine countries, experienced, knowledgeable guides can be found in most mountain towns. Guides are accredited by the Compañia de Guías de Montaña of the F.E.M. A list of these guides and their addresses appears in the *F.E.M. Annuario* (see the section on Spain's Walking clubs). Their addresses may also be obtained from the F.E.M. (see *Address Directory*). If you write to the F.E.M. for their addresses, be sure to specify the mountain region in which you wish to climb and, if possible, the specific peaks which are of interest to you and the name of the town which you plan to use as a base.

Mountaineering Courses

Mountaineering courses are offered to F.E.M. members by the F.E.M.'s Escuela Nacional de Alta Montaña—the national mountaineering school—which has several sections operating in various parts of Spain. Courses are available in rock climbing, winter climbing and advanced mountaineering. There are also courses for beginners and for groups. For further information you may write the F.E.M., the regional mountaineering federations or:

> **Escuela Nacional de Alta Montaña** (see *Address Directory*). Correspondence should be in Catalan or Spanish.

Cross-Country Skiing & Ski Mountaineering

Of the more than 300,000 skiers in Spain, perhaps only 2,000 engage in cross-country skiing. There are very few established cross-country ski tracks, and these are mostly for competitive events and are taken down afterwards. Nevertheless, the mountains of Spain offer numerous opportunities for cross-country skiing and ski mountaineering, especially in the vicinity of the established downhill ski resorts.

Sixteen guidebooks currently exist to ski touring and ski mountaineering in the Pyrenees and another 16 titles are planned (see the section on Guidebooks). But in the rest of Spain you are still very much on your own. You must bring your own equipment and figure out your own routes. Also, because no ski maps are available, you should always carry the appropriate 1:50,000 topographical maps and a good compass.

It is possible to ski in the mountains of Spain from December through March and on some high, north-facing slopes until mid-June. Ski facilities are best developed in the Pyrenees, where there are almost 20 ski resorts. There are also ski areas in the Cordillera Cantábrica, the Sistema Ibérico, the Sierra de Guadarrama, the Sierra Nevada and other areas. For information on cross-country skiing in the vicinity of the various ski resorts, you should contact each resort individually. The resorts are listed below. Their addresses and telephone numbers, including the telephone numbers to call for snow condition reports, appear in the *Address Directory:*

Cordillera Cantábrica

Alto Campoo: Cantur, Santander.

Cabeza de Manzaneda: Estación de Invierno (Mieso), Manzaneda (Orense).

Pajares: Diputación Provincial de Oviedo, Oviedo.

Puerto de San Isidro: Diputación Provincial de León, León.

Trevinca: Montañas de Trevinca, S.A., Vigo (Pontevedra) and Barco de Valdeorras (Orense).

Pyrenees (Aragon)

Candanchu: Explotaciones Turisticas de Candanchu (Etuksa), Candanchu (Huesca).

Cerler: Cerler, Barcelona.

El Formigal: Formigal S.A., Zaragoza.

Panticosa: Panticosa Turistica, Zaragoza.

Valle de Astun: Estación Invernal Valle de Astun, S.A., Zaragoza.

Pyrenees (Catalunya)

Baqueira-Beret: Oficina de Turismo de Baqueira-Beret, Alto Aran, Pirineos (Lérida) and Baqueira-Beret, S.A., Barcelona.

Bohi-Tahull: Promociones Turisticas del Pirineo, S.A., Barcelona.

Lles de Cerdanya: Lles de Cerdanya, Lles (Lérida).

Llessui: Pallars Turistico, Barcelona.

Masella: Masella, Barcelona.

Nuria: Ferrocariles de Montaña de Grandes Pendientes, Barcelona.

Port del Comte: Port del Comte, Solsona (Lérida).

Sant Joan de L'Erm: Pistas Sant Joan de L'Erm, Seo de Urgel (Lérida).

Super-Espot: Super-Espot, Barcelona. Conducts guided ski touring and ski mountaineering excursions in the Parc Nacional de Sant Maurici.

Tuca, Valle de Aran: Tuca, Viella (Lérida) and Barcelona.

Rasos de Peguera-Ensija: Ensija, Berga (Barcelona).
Valle de la Molina: Telesquis Pirenaicos, Barcelona.
Vall-Ter-2000: Vall Ter S.A., Camprodon (Gerona).

Sierra Nevada

Sierra Nevada: Cetursa, Granada.

Sistema Central

La Pinilla: La Pinilla, Madrid 16. Located in the Sierra de Ayllon.
Puerto de Navacerrada: Transportes Aereos del Guadarrama, Madrid. Located in the Sierra de Guadarrama.
Valcotos: Transportes Aereos del Guadarrama, Madrid. Located in the Sierra de Guadarrama.
Valdesquí: Estación Alpina de Cotos, Madrid. Located in the Sierra de Guadarrama.

Sistema Ibérico

Estación de Valdezcaray: Valdezcaray, S.A., Ezcaray (Logroño). Located in the mountains south of Logroño.
Sierra de Gudar: Eskamp, S.L., Valencia. Located in the mountains near Teruel.

Detailed descriptions of Spain's principal skiing regions and their resorts are contained in two valuable guidebooks:

- *Guide: Winter Resorts* (in English) by Rafael Pellús de Basaldúa, Secretaria de Estado del Turismo, Madrid, 1972. An excellent guide to the major ski resorts in Spain, with numerous color photographs of each ski area. Introductions describe each skiing district, show its location and include an elevational cross section of the district. Sketch maps show the location of each ski resort as well as each of its lifts and runs. The descriptions of each resort provide information on: 1) access via road, railway and air; 2) distance from major cities; 3) altitude; 4) number of marked runs; 5) technical data on each lift; 6) the locations, altitude and details on where keys can be obtained for nearby refuges; 7) where to obtain medical assistance; 8) lodgings; and 9) miscellaneous information on climate, flora and fauna, possible excursions and other matters of interest. A large section at the end of the guide discusses: 1) resort safety regulations; 2) the Escuela Española de Esqui (the Spanish Ski School); 3) accident procedures; 4) rules for alpine skiing competitions; 5) equipment (including cross-country) and other matters of interest.

The section also lists the names, addresses and telephone numbers of mountain guides, regional skiing federations, regional and provincial mountaineering federations, mountain rescue services, tourist offices abroad and tourist information offices in Spain. Available for a nominal charge from the Llibreria Quera (see Address Directory). Recommended.

- *Winter Sports: Spain* (in English), Secretaria de Estado del Turismo, Madrid, 1975. Contains much of the same information as the above publication, although not in such great detail. Free from most tourist information offices throughout Spain.

Cross-country skiing and ski mountaineering is overseen in Spain by F.E.M.'s Comité de Esqui de Montaña. For information on where to ski, you should contact the local committee president for each of the regional and provincial mountaineering federations (see *Address Directory*).

The Comité de Esqui de Montaña recommends the following mountain regions and routes for ski touring and ski mountaineering:

Sistema Central

Sierra de Guadarrama: 1) from Puerto de Navacerrada to Puerto de la Morcuera (one-day trip); 2) from Puerto de Cotos to Puerto de Navafria (one-day trip).

Sierra de Gredos: Several routes of various durations are possible, including a two-to-three-day traverse along the crest of the range. The route can be extended to the Sierra de Bejar. Several ascents are possible from the refuge in the Circo de Gredos.

Cordillera Cantábrica

Peña Ubiña: Several possible routes.

Picos de Europa: The central, eastern and western massifs offer a variety of routes ranging from one to several days in duration. A traverse of all three massifs takes from three to five days, with stops at the refuges of Naranjo de Bulnes, Cabaña Veronica, Collado Jermoso and Peñas Santas.

Pyrenees

The Pyrenees offer endless opportunities for ski touring, including a traverse of the entire range. Several routes of varying duration are possible in each of the following areas.

Benasque: The finest area in the Pyrenees for cross-country skiing, offering excellent terrain and snow conditions. Possible routes include: 1) ascent of

Aneto, the highest peak in the Pyrenees, from the Refugio de la Renclusa, near Benasque (two-day trip); 2) ascent of the massif of Las Maladetas from the same refuge; 3) from Benasque to Valle de Estós, the Valle de Arán or the Posets Massif; 4) ascent of the Posets Massif via Viadós; descent to Benasque via the Valle de Estós; refuges at Viadós and Valle de Estós (two-day trip).

Candanchú and the headwaters of the Río Aragón: Several possible routes.

Goriz and Monte Perdido: Several possible ascents of the massif of Monte Perdido and of the Marboré peaks. Routes also exist in the Valle de Ordesa and the Valle del rio Ara. Refuges at Goriz and Serradets.

Piedrafita and Panticosa: Several ascents are possible from Sallent de Gállego by way of the refuge at Piedrafita. Extended trips can be taken toward Panticosa or the massif of Vignemale.

Valles de Roncal (Navarra), Ansó and Hecho (Aragón): Possible ascents to the Mesa de los Tres Reyes, Anie, Petrechema, Visurin and other places.

Valle de Aran: Numerous routes possible near the Valle de Aran, Parque Nacional de Aigües Tortes-Lago San Mauricio La Molina, Nuria and in the tiny country of Andorra.

Sierra Nevada

Numerous routes are possible from the Estación de Esquí Sol y Nieve, including ascents of Mulhacén (the highest peak in the Iberian Peninsula), Veleta, Alcazaba and other peaks.

Trains & Buses

Although you can take a train or bus almost anywhere in Spain, service is notoriously slow. Many of the trains and railway beds are in poor condition, and the resulting lurching, jostling ride can strain your patience, if not an occasional muscle. Spain has several high-speed luxury trains known as *Talgos*. Fares on these first-class-only trains are steep in comparison to regular train fares, but more than worth every peseta, especially if you are traveling a long distance. Problem is, the number of *Talgos* is limited, and they are confined to the principal long-distance runs, such as Barcelona-Madrid. The rest of the trains will get you to your destination, but you should be prepared for a long and sometimes tiring trip. When you have a choice, choose a TER or TAF. These are much faster and more comfortable than the *expressos*. Although the *expresso* may not entirely live up to its name, it will be considerably faster than a *rapido*. The *correo*, on the other hand, is best saved for short trips; these trains stop at every place anyone could conceivably want to get on or off.

Spanish buses are very economical and will drop you off almost anywhere you wish. Generally, their schedules are posted in train and bus stations or, in villages lacking a train station, in the post office. The buses provide excellent access to Spain's mountain areas. But it is advisable to get as close as possible to your hiking destination by train before switching to the buses. They, like the *correo*, can make a long trip seem even longer.

RENFE, the Spanish national railway, offers several special discounts on so-called *días azules* (blue days), of which there were 306 in 1980. These discounts include:

1. A 50 percent discount for persons 65 years of age or older, and

2. A 25 percent discount for groups of 10 people or more.

You can also purchase a train ticket checkbook—called *Chequetren*—that contains coupons good for rail travel at a savings of 15 percent or more off regular fares. The coupons are exchanged at ticket windows for regular tickets as you need them. There is no time limit within which you must use the coupons. Up to six people can also travel on the same pass. *Chequetren* can be purchased only in Spain.

Travelers should be aware that hitchhiking is strictly illegal in Spain. Violation can mean a substantial fine, short jail sentence or deportation as an undesirable alien. To add to this, traffic is sparse outside the major cities, the waits long and, in summer, the Spanish sun broiling.

Useful Addresses & Telephone Numbers

General Tourist Information

In Spain:

Secretaria de Estado del Turismo (see *Address Directory*). When requesting publications, address your enquiry to the *Gabinete de Publicaciones*.

There is a tourist information office in every city and major town in Spain that can supply information on the surrounding region. A list of addresses is available on request from the Secretaria de Estado del Turismo.

Abroad:

The Spanish National Tourist Office has branch offices in: EUROPE: Brussels, Copenhagen, Düsseldorf, Frankfurt, Geneva, Hamburg, Helsinki, The Hague, Lisbon, London, Milan, Munich, Oslo, Paris, Rome, Vienna and Zurich; JAPAN: Tokyo; CANADA: Toronto; and the U.S.A.: Chicago, San Francisco and New York.

London: Spanish National Tourist Office, 57-58 St. James Street, London SW1A 1LD. Tel. (01) 499 1095 or 499 0901.

New York: Spanish National Tourist Office, 665 Fifth Avenue, New York, New York 10022. Tel. (212) 759-8822.

Sport Shops

The following sport shops offer limited selections of walking and mountaineering equipment:

See *Address Directory*:

Diez Deportes. Four locations in Madrid.

La Flecha de Oro. Two locations in Madrid.

El Sherpa. Two locations in Madrid.

Puigmal, in Barcelona.

Sanjust, in Barcelona.

Sports Alp, in Barcelona.

Bookstores

See *Address Directory*:

Libreria Deportiva, in Madrid. Stocks a small selection of books on walking and mountaineering, including the Everest guides and the Editorial Alpina map-guides. Does not sell walking maps.

Libreria Esteban Sanz, also in Madrid.

Libreria Gema, in Oviedo.

Llibreria Quera in Barcelona. Stocks the most complete selection of walking guides, maps and books on walking and mountaineering in Spain.

Search & Rescue

Search and rescue in Spain is carried out either by volunteer groups or by the local police. Victims must bear the costs of search and rescue operations; insurance covering these costs is therefore advisable. F.E.M. membership includes complete insurance coverage.

> **In case of emergency:** Find the nearest telephone and call the local *Guardia Civil* (the number will be listed in the front pages of the telephone directory).

As an alternative, you can call the appropriate provincial or regional mountaineering federation (for their telephone numbers, see the *Address Directory* at the end of this chapter). It is generally quicker, however, to call the Guardia Civil.

LONG DISTANCE FOOTPATHS IN CATALANA

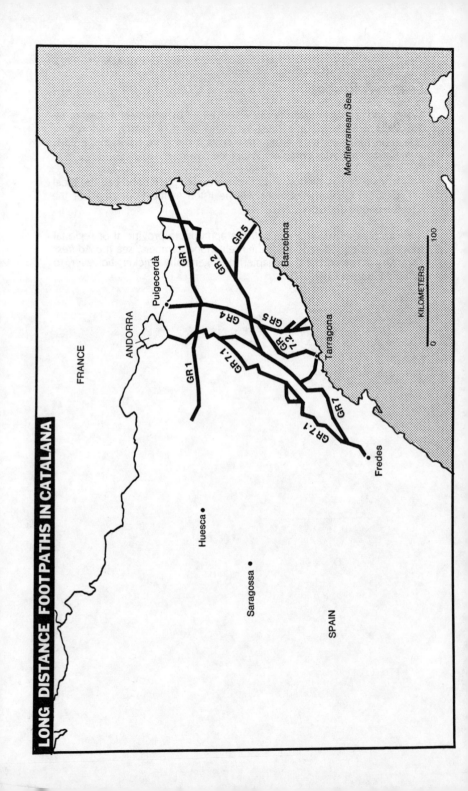

Spain's Long-Distance Footpaths

Although you can piece together extended walks in the Spanish mountains—especially the Pyrenees—by linking up a number of shorter paths, Spain has very few official long-distance footpaths. And those that exist are largely confined to Catalunya, which can probably boast of more active walking clubs and enthusiastic walkers and mountaineers than any other region in Spain.

At present, there are about 1,200 kilometers of marked long-distance footpaths in Catalunya, comprised primarily of G.R. (Gran Recorregut) 4, which runs from Puicerdà, on the French border in the Pyrenees, to Montserrat—a distance of 125 kilometers (78 miles)—and G.R. 7, which runs from Andorra, in the Pyrenees, to the town of Fredes, north of Valencia—a distance of 363 kilometers (225 miles). G.R. 7 also includes four marked alternate routes—G.R. 7-1, G.R. 7-2, G.R. 7-3 and G.R. 7-4—which have a combined length of about 500 kilometers. In addition, several other long-distance footpaths are currently being marked in the region. These include: 1) G.R. 1 from Port Bou on the Costa Brava in Girona, running west through Albanyá, St. Pau de Seguries, Ripoll, La Quar, Berga, St. Llorenç and Tremp to the border of Huesca province; 2) G.R. 2 from La Jonquera in the Pyrenees, running south through Besalú, Sta. Pau, Tavertet, Vilanove de Sau, Seva and Centelles to St. Quirze Safaja, north of Barcelona; and 3) G.R. 5 from Sant Pol on the coast north of Barcelona, running west through Aiguafreda and St. Quirze Safaja, then south through St. Llorenç de Munt, Montserrat and Vendrell to the Costa Dorado south of Barcelona.

Catalunya's long-distance footpaths are overseen by:

Comité Catalá de Senders de Gran Recorregut (see *Address Directory*). Responsible for planning and marking Catalunya's long-distance footpaths. Works closely with Catalunya's local clubs and the Comités de Senderos de Gran Recorrido (long-distance footpath committees) of all the Spanish mountaineering federations. Represents Spain on the Walking Committee of the European Ramblers' Association. Can provide information on Catalunya's long-distance footpaths, both complete and in project. Conducts walking tours on sections of the various long-distance footpaths. Also publishes leaflets describing these tours in Catalan, Spanish, English and French. Staff speaks Catalan, Spanish and some French. Responses are usually thorough and prompt.

European Long-Distance Footpath E-4 enters Spain at Puicerdà and follows G.R. 4 to Montserrat, G.R. 7-2 (an alternate route of G.R. 7) from Montserrat to Bellprat and G.R. 7 from Bellprat to Fredes—a distance of

368 kilometers (229 miles). The entire route is marked with red and white horizontal bars. Within the next year the path is expected to be extended southward all the way to Gibraltar.

G.R. 7

A continuation of France's G.R. 7. From la Seu d'Urgell, near the Andorran border, to Fredes. Down the southern slope of the eastern Pyrenees and across Catalunya, with its gently rolling hills covered with pines, cork oaks, figs and olive groves. Enroute, river valleys flanked by fields; successive ranges of mountains with peaks of red and yellow rocks; stucco-walled villages; and lone herders tending flocks of sheep. In addition to the main route, there are four marked alternative routes of varying lengths: 1) G.R. 7-1 from Pinós to Paüls; roughly parallels the route of G.R. 7 to the west; 2) G.R. 7-2 from Bellprat to La Mussara; heads northeast to Montserrat, swings south to Tarragona on the Costa Dorado, then curves east through Reus to rejoin G.R. 7 between Mont-ral and Arboli; adds many kilometers to the route; 3) G.R. 7-3 a short alternate route between Argentera and Llaveria: and 4) G.R. 7-4 a short alternate route from Montblanc to Clot del Llop. **Length:** 363 kilometers (G.R. 7 only). **Walking Time:** 14 days. **Difficulty:** Easy to moderately difficult. **Path Markings:** White and red horizontal bars (alternative routes are also marked).

Trail Lodgings: In La Seu d'Urgell, five hotels; in La Coma, one hotel; in Sant Llorenç de Morunys, one hotel; in Solsona, one hotel and one guesthouse; in Santuari Miracle, one hotel; in Santa Coloma de Queralt, one guesthouse; in Miramar, one refuge; in Coli de Lilla, one hotel; in Mont-ral, one refuge; in Argentera, one guesthouse; in Tivissa, one guesthouse; in Benifallet, one guesthouse; in Paüls, one guesthouse; and in Caro, one refuge. Lodgings *must* be arranged in advance in the following three refuges: (see *Address Directory*).
Refugio del AAEEMI. Located in Miramar.
Refugio Musté-Recasens. Located in Mont-ral. Maintained by the Seccion Excursionista del Centro de Lectura de Reus.
Refugio Caro. Located between Paüls and Fredes. For information, write the Unió Excursionista de Catalunya, Tortosa. Additional information on lodging is available from the Oficina de Información de Turismo, Barcelona.

Maps:
- *G.R. 7:* Instituto Geográfico Nacional Mapa Topográfico 1:50,000, sheets 215, 216, 253, 254, 292, 330, 362, 390, 391, 418, 445, 446, 471, 472, 497, 521, 522 and 546.
- *G.R. 7-1:* Instituto Geográfico Nacional Mapa Topográfico 1:50,000, sheets 330, 361, 362, 390, 417, 418, 444, 445, 470, 471, 496 and 521.
- *G.R. 7-2:* Instituto Geográfico Nacional Mapa Topográfico 1:50,000, sheets 363, 390, 391, 392, 418, 419, 445, 446, 472 and 473.

- *G.R. 7-3:* Instituto Geográfico Nacional Mapa Topográfico 1:50,000, sheet 471.
- *G.R. 7-4:* Instituto Geográfico Nacional Mapa Topográfico 1:50,000, sheets 417 and 418.

Guidebooks:
- *Topo-Guia G.R. 7:* Seven volumes: 1) *de la Seu d'Urgell al Santuari del Miracle,* 2) *del Santuari del Miracle a Bellprat,* 3) *de Bellprat a la Riba,* 4) *de la Riba al coll de la Teixeta,* 5) *del coll de la Teixeta a Tivissa,* 6) *de Tivissa a Paüls* and 7) *de Paüls a Fredes* (in both Spanish and Catalan), Editorial SERPA. Only volumes 5, 6, and 7 have so far been published. Available from Editorial SERPA or Llibreria Quera. (see *Address Directory*).
- *Els Senders de Gran Recorregut de les Comarques Tarragonines* (in Catalan), edited by l'Assemblea d'Entitats Escursionistes de les Comarques Meridionals de Catalunya. Sketch map showing marked footpaths in the region surrounding Tarragona. G.R. 7 from Solsona to Fredes, along with G.R. 7-1, G.R. 7-2, G.R. 7-3 and G.R. 7-4, are shown by solid red lines. G.R. 5 (in the process of being marked) is shown by a broken red line. Short paths branching off from the main routes or linking them are shown by solid yellow lines. Includes a pictorial key showing path markings and a list of bookstores where Editorial SERPA Topo-Guias to G.R. 7 may be purchased. This map is useful for planning your route but is unsuited for finding your way along the various paths. Available from Comité Catalá de Senders de Gran Recorregut (see *Address Directory*).
- *Descripción del G.R. 7-1* (in Catalan). Describes G.R. 7-1 from Pinós to Prades (about half the full route). Available from Editorial SERPA or Llibreria Quera (see *Address Directory*)

G.R. 4

From Puicerdà to Montserrat. Part of European Long-Distance Footpath E-4. South through the eastern Pyrenees and rolling hills of Catalunya. This path was completed in June, 1979. **Length:** 125 kilometers. **Walking Time:** One week. **Difficulty:** Easy to moderately difficult. **Path Markings:** Red and white horizontal bars.

Trail Lodgings: In the mountains, three hotels; in Pobla de Lillet, two hotels; in Borreda, two hotels; in La Guardia, one small inn; in Manresa, various hotels; and in Montserrat, various hotels.

Maps:
- Instituto Geográfico Nacional Mapa Topográfico 1:50,000, sheets 217, 255, 293, 331, 363 and 392.

Guidebooks:
- *Descripción del G-R 4* (in Catalan). A provisional route description covering G.R. 4. Available from the Comité Catalá de Senders de Gran Recorregut of Llibreria Quera (see *Address Directory*).

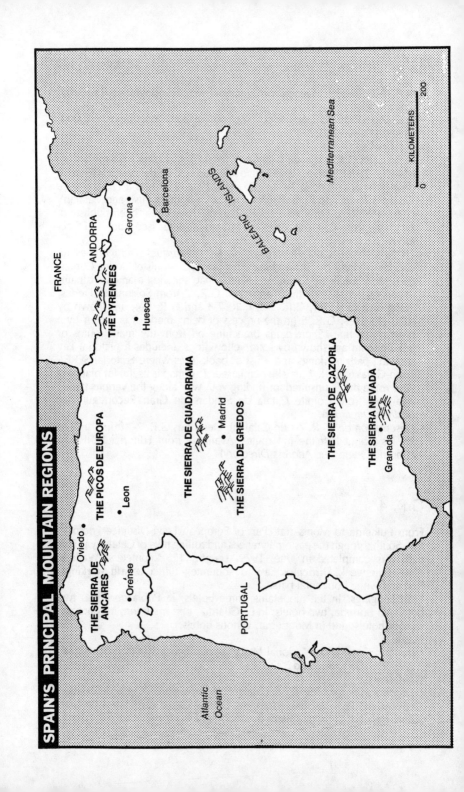

SPAIN'S PRINCIPAL MOUNTAIN REGIONS

Spain's Principal Walking Regions

The several great mountain chains—*cordillera* or *sistema*—marching across Spain constitute its principal walking regions. Each cordillera is composed of several *sierras*—individual ranges of mountains or hills. Although it is possible to walk throughout much of Spain on country lanes and rural tracks, it is the sierras, with their wild beauty, numerous footpaths and scattered refuges, that are of greatest interest to most walkers.

Catalunya

Catalunya lies in Spain's extreme northeastern corner, forming a rough triangle made up of the provinces of Lérida, Girona, Barcelona and Tarragona. It is best known, perhaps, for the historic and cosmopolitan city of Barcelona, the second largest in Spain, and for its sunny resort coasts—the Costa Dorada and Costa Brava—with their wooded headlands, coves and white-sand beaches. The region also includes the eastern half of the Spanish Pyrenees (which are discussed separately in the section on *The Pyrennes*). On the south, near the city of Lérida, spreads the broad, fertile valley of the Río Ebro, with its farming villages and irrigated fields.

Most of the region, however, is covered with a complex system of low wooded ridges and intervening valleys. These hills are, in fact, the foothills of the Pyrenees, which rise to the north. Covered with woodlands of pine and cork oak, with scattered groves of fig and olive trees, the ridges seldom exceed 1,000 meters (3,280 feet) in elevation and are often much lower.

Numerous footpaths crisscross the region, including several marked long-distance routes (see above). Portions of three of these—G.R. 4, G.R. 7 and G.R. 7-2—link up to form the southernmost segment of European Long-Distance Footpath E-4. Several other long-distance paths are now being marked. Walks are also possible on numerous unmarked footpaths and quiet country lanes. It is possible to walk throughout the year in the Catalunyan hills, and whatever season you choose your visit will be rewarded by pleasant woodlands, cool streams and pleasant rural villages.

Catalunya derives its identity, however, not from geography or terrain, but from its distinctive language and culture. The native tongue is not the Castilian Spanish spoken throughout the rest of Spain, but Catalan, a separate language.

Catalunya is rich in history and tradition. The city of Tarragona existed as early as 218 B.C. and was made the capital of the province by Julius Caesar. The first bishop of Barcelona took up residence in the third century A.D. Medieval castles and churches—some still standing, some in ruins—are scattered throughout the region. Village fiestas, held to commemorate the feast days of patron saints, as well as various other occasions, occur throughout the year, with dances, parades, pilgrimages, religious rites, sporting events and other forms of traditional pageantry.

Useful Addresses

Federació d'Entitats Excurisionistes de Catalunya (Federación Catalana de Montañismo). See *Address Directory*. Can provide a list of its publications, information on the location of refuges, walking, climbing, ski mountaineering and cave exploration throughout Catalunya. Can also provide information on walking and climbing tours and other activities by the federation and its affiliated clubs. Affiliated with 145 clubs devoted to mountaineering, skiing and other activities. Staff speaks Catalan and Spanish.

The following tourist offices can provide general information on their respective provinces, including lodging lists, road maps and brochures describing features of interest. Their addresses and telephone numbers are listed in the *Address Directory* at the end of this chapter.

Barcelona: Oficina de Información de Turismo. Staff speaks Catalan, Spanish, French, limited English and some German.

Gerona: Oficina de Información de Turismo, Gerona. Staff speaks Catalan, Spanish, French and limited English.

Lérida: Oficina de Información de Turismo, Lérida. Staff speaks Catalan, Spanish and French.

Tarragona: Oficina de Información de Turismo, Tarragona. Staff speaks Catalan, Spanish and French.

Maps

Catalunya (including the Pyrenees) are covered by the following topographical maps:

Barcelona Province: Instituto Geográfico Nacional Mapa Topográfico 1:50,000, sheets 254, 255, 292, 293, 294, 330, 331, 332, 361, 362, 363, 364, 365, 390, 391, 392, 393, 394, 419, 420, 421, 447 and 448.

Gerona Province: Instituto Geográfico Nacional Mapa Topográfico 1:50,000, sheets 216, 217, 218, 219, 220, 221, 255, 256, 257, 258, 259, 293, 294, 295, 296, 297, 332, 333, 334, 335, 364, 365 and 366.

Lérida Province: Instituto Geográfico Nacional Mapa Topográfico 1:50,000, sheets 118 bis., 148, 149, 150, 180, 181, 182, 213, 214, 215, 216, 251, 252, 253, 254, 289, 290, 291, 292, 327, 328, 329, 330, 358, 359, 360, 361, 387, 388, 389, 390, 415, 416, 417 and 443.

Tarragona Province: Instituto Geográfico Nacional Mapa Topográfico 1:50,000, sheets 390, 417, 418, 443, 444, 445, 447, 470, 471, 472, 473, 496, 497, 498, 521, 522, 523, 546 and 547.

Costa Brava (Gerona): Instituto Geográfico Nacional Mapa Topográfico 1:50,000, sheets 220, 221, 258, 296, 297, 334, 335 and 366.

Costa Dorado (Barcelona): Instituto Geográfico Nacional Mapa Topográfico 1:50,000, sheets 393, 394, 420, 421, 447 and 448.

Costa Dorado (Tarragona): Instituto Geográfico Nacional Mapa Topográfico 1:50,000, sheets 446, 447, 472, 473, 497, 498, 522, 523 and 547.

Pyrenees: Instituto Geográfico Nacional Mapa Topográfico 1:50,000, sheets 118 bis., 148, 149, 150, 180, 181, 182, 183 (covers part of Andorra), 213, 214, 215, 216 (covers part of Andorra), 217, 218, 219, 220, 253, 254, 255, 256, 257, 292 and 293.

Guidebooks

For details on guidebooks and map-guides to walks and climbs in Catalunya, see the section on *Guidebooks* earlier in this chapter. In addition to the guidebooks listed for Catalunya, the following is also useful:

- *Bergwelt Spaniens* (in German) by Agustin Jolis, Fink-Kümmerly + Frey, Stuttgart, 1973. Describes eight walks around Montserrat northwest of Barcelona, four walks around Montseny between Barcelona and Tarragona and 18 walks in the Catalan Pyrenees. Available from GEO CENTER (see *Address Directory*).

A price list, as well as a list of other guidebooks, map-guides and *fichas* (or leaflets) covering the footpaths in Catalunya can be obtained upon request from Llibreria Quera.

Suggested Walks

Numerous walks, both short and long, are possible in the foothills of Catalunya. Three recommendations are along long-distance footpaths G.R. 7 and its alternate G.R. 7-2 and along G.R. 4 (see the section on *Spain's Long Distance Footpaths*). All three paths lend themselves to being walked in shorter sections, and several interconnecting trails make a number of circuits possible.

The Cordillera Cantábrica

The Cordillera Cantábrica is a vast mountain system stretching across northern Spain from the Pyrenees in the east to the mountains of Galicia in the west—a distance of more than 400 kilometers (250 miles). The mountains, made up of numerous individual ranges, parallel Spain's northern coast—the Cornisa Cantábrica—and lie inland only 20 to 40 kilometers.

Numerous footpaths, most of them unmarked, are found throughout the Cordillera Cantábrica. They climb through lush woodlands of oak, beech, chestnut, ash and birch; follow tumbling streams carving their way through deep, rocky gorges; cross great alpine pastures above tree limit; ascend high, barren passes from which the views of distant peaks and valleys, and even the sea, are spectacular; and wander through pleasant valleys dotted with farms and quaint mountain villages.

Numerous refuges are scattered throughout the central and western portions of the cordillera. Accommodation is also easily obtained throughout the range in the larger towns and villages nestled in the mountains.

Several groups of peaks rising above 2,000 meters are scattered in the western and, especially, the central parts of the range. These include the peaks of Alto Carrion and the Sierra de Peña Labra, in the province of Palencia; of Alto Campoo and the Sierra de Peña Sagra, in the province of Santander; of the Macizo de Peña Ubiña, in the province of Oviedo, and of the Montes de Riaño, in the province of León.

By far the greatest of the many ranges comprising the Cordillera

Cantábrica, however, is the group of three massifs known together as the Picos de Europa, which straddle the borders of Oviedo, Santander and León provinces. These great limestone massifs are separated by profound chasms carved through the mountains by the Cares and Duje rivers. The peaks on either side of these gorges rise more than 2,000 meters above the rivers, culminating in spectacular arrays of jagged, snowy summits. Numerous peaks exceeding 2,000 meters elevation beckon the mountaineer, and several are accessible only to technical climbers. Numerous footpaths, most of them unmarked, are found in all three massifs. There are also several refuges, including two national paradores. The Parque Nacional de las Montañas de Covadonga includes most of the Macizo Occidental—the western massif—providing refuge for chamois, roebuck, wild boar, Pyrenees bears and wolves. Natural reserves are located in the Macizo Central and Oriental. The highest peaks are found in the Macizo Central, where three exceed 2,600 meters elevation. Much of the Picos de Europa is roadless, accessible only to the walker and climber.

East of Reinosa and Alto Campoo, in the province of Santander, the ranges of the Cordillera Cantábrica diminish in stature, with few peaks approaching 2,000 meters elevation. This part of the system stretches eastward through Burgos and the Basque provinces of Alava, Vizcaya and Guipúzcoa to merge imperceptibly with the Navarran Pyrenees. Numerous walks are possible in these rocky, wooded ranges—known collectively as the Montes Vascos—which include the Sierra de Aralar, Sierra de Cantábra and Montes de Vittoria, to name but a few.

Useful Addresses

The following mountaineering federations can provide information on walking, climbing, ski mountaineering and cave exploration in their provinces. They can also provide lists of their publications, information on the locations of mountain refuges, and schedules of the walking and climbing tours, mountaineering courses and other activities which they and their affiliated local clubs organize. Before writing the clubs, however, it is advisable to read the section on *Where to Get Walking Information* to ensure a better chance of a response.

See *Address Directory*:

Federación Asturiana de Montañismo. Oversees mountaineering activities in the province of Oviedo (Asturias). Affiliated with 41 local clubs devoted to mountaineering and skiing. Staff speaks Spanish.

Federación Cantabra de Montañismo. Oversees mountaineering activities in the province of Santander. Affiliated with 14 local clubs devoted to mountaineering and cave exploration. Staff speaks Spanish.

Federación Castellana de Montañismo. Oversees mountaineering activities in Castile and Extremadura. Of its affiliated clubs, 13 are located in the province of Burgos. Staff speaks Spanish. A few staff members also speak some French and English.

Federación Leonesa de Montañismo. Oversees mountaineering activities in the province of León. Affiliated with 18 local clubs devoted to mountaineering and cave exploration. Staff speaks Spanish.

Federación Palentina de Montañismo. Oversees mountaineering activities in the province of Palencia. Affiliated with 14 local clubs devoted to mountaineering and cave exploration. Staff speaks Spanish.

Federación Vasco-Navarra de Montañismo. Oversees mountaineering activities in the Basque provinces of Alava, Guipúzcoa and Vizcaya, as well as in the province of Navarra. Affiliated with 145 local clubs devoted to mountaineering, skiing, cave exploration and other activities. Staff speaks Euskara and Spanish.

The following tourist offices can provide general information on their respective provinces, including lodging lists, road maps and brochures describing features of interest. For their addresses and telephone numbers, see the *Address Directory.*

Alava: Oficina de Información de Turismo, Vitoria. Staff speaks Euskara and Spanish.

Burgos: Oficina de Información de Turismo, Burgos. Staff speaks Spanish.

Guipúzcoa: Oficina de Información de Turismo, San Sebastián. Staff speaks Euskara and Spanish.

León: Oficina de Información de Turismo, León. Staff speaks Spanish.

Oviedo (Asturias): Oficina de Información de Turismo, Oviedo. Staff speaks Spanish.

Palencia: Oficina de Informatión de Turismo, Palencia. Staff speaks Spanish.

Santander: Oficina de Información de Turismo, Santander. Staff speaks Spanish and French.

Vizcaya: Oficina de Información de Turismo, Bilbao. Staff speaks Euskara and Spanish.

Maps

The various ranges of the Cordillera Cantábrica are covered by the following topographical maps:

Alava Province: Instituto Geográfico Nacional Mapa Topográfico 1:50,000, sheets 86, 87, 111, 112, 113, 137, 138, 139, 170 and 171.

Burgos Province: Instituto Geográfico Nacional Mapa Topográfico 1:50,000, sheets 84, 85, 108, 109, 110, 111, 134, 135, 136, 137, 165, 166, 167, 168 and 169.

Guipúzcoa Province: Instituto Geográfico Nacional Mapa Topográfico 1:50,000, sheets 41, 63, 64, 65, 88, 89, 113 and 114.

León Province (including the Montes de Riaño and Picos de Europa): Instituto Geográfico Nacional Mapa Topográfico 1:50,000, sheets 55, 70, 80, 81, 100, 101, 102, 103, 104, 105, 106, 125, 126, 127, 128, 129, 130, 131, 157, 158, 159, 160, 161, 162, and 163.

Oviedo Province (including the Macizo de Peña Ubiña and Picos de Europa): Instituto Geográfico Nacional Mapa Topográfico 1:50,000, sheets 50, 51, 52, 53, 54, 55, 56, 75, 76, 77, 78, 79, 80, 100 and 101.

Palencia Province (including the Alto Carrion, Sierra de Peña Labra and Picos de Europa): Instituto Geográfico Nacional Mapa Topográfico 1:50,000, sheets 81, 82, 106, 107, 131, 132, 133, 134, 163, 164 and 165.

Santander Province (including the Alto Campoo, Sierra de Peña Sagra and Picos de Europa): Instituto Geográfico Nacional Mapa Topográfico 1:50,000, sheets 34, 35, 36, 56, 57, 58, 59, 60, 81, 82, 83, 84, 107, 108 and 134.

Vizcaya Province: Instituto Geográfico Nacional Mapa Topográfico 1:50,000, sheets 37, 38, 60, 61, 62, 63, 86 and 87.

Picos de Europa: Instituto Geográfico Nacional Mapa Topográfico 1:50,000, sheets 55, 56, 57, 80, 81, 82, 105, 106 and 107.

Guidebooks & Map-Guides

For details on the guidebooks and map-guides covering the Cordillera Cantábrica see the sections on *Maps* and *Guidebooks* earlier in this chapter. In addition to the guidebooks listed for the Cordillera Cantábrica, the following is also useful:

- *Bergwelt Spaniens* (in German) by Agustin Jolis, Fink-Kümmerly + Frey, Stuttgart, 1973. Describes 13 walks in the Montes Vascos, 8 walks in the Macizo de Peña Ubiña and 16 walks in the Picos de Europa. Available from GEO CENTER.

A price list, as well as a list of other guidebooks, map-guides and *fichas* (or leaflets) covering the footpaths in the Cordillera Cantábrica can be obtained upon request from Llibreria Quera, Libreria Gema and the individual mountaineering federations.

Suggested Walks

Numerous walks are possible in the Cordillera Cantábrica. Although there are no official long-distance footpaths in these mountains, shorter routes can often be linked up for longer excursions by referring to the appropriate topographical maps and map-guides. Some recommended day-long walks are:

From Refugio de Vega Redonda to Refugio de Llago Huerta and return. A circuit through the heart of the Macizo Occidental of the Picos de Europa, providing spectacular close-up views of Peña Santa, highest peak in the massif. The route crosses five passes and has two short cross-country sections. Across meadows, alongside lakes and below a grand array of imposing crags. **Walking Time:** 6 hours. **Difficulty:** Moderately difficult to difficult. **Path Markings:** None.

Special Note: Access to the Refugio de Vega Redonda is by way of a footpath from Vega la Piedra, which is located at the end of the road leading from Covadonga to Lago Enol. At the lake, take the right fork of the road south for a couple of kilometers to a second junction. Turn left and continue to the end of the road. The track leading to the Refugio de Vega Redonda begins here. Approximate walking time to the refuge: one hour.

Maps:
• Instituto Geográfico Nacional Mapa Topográfico 1:50,000, sheet 55 *Beleño.*

Path Description:
• *Picos de Europa, I: Macizo Occidental* (in Spanish). Available from Llibreria Quera.

From Puente Pocebos to Horcadina de Cobarrobres. A grand north-south crossing of the Macizo Central of the Picos de Europa. Through meadows, alongside streams, past mountain tarns and over the high pass at Las Urrieles. Awesome, close-up views of the highest peaks in the range, including spectacular Naranjo de Bulnes, a favorite objective of climbers. **Walking Time:** 8 to 9 hours; best to take two days. **Difficulty:** Moderately difficult to difficult. **Path Markings:** None.

Maps:
• Instituto Geográfico Nacional Mapa Topográfico 1:50,000, sheets 81 *Potes* and 106 *Camporredondo de Alba.*

Path Descriptions:
• *Bergwelt Spaniens* (in German). Available from GEO CENTER.
• *Picos de Europa, II: Naranjo de Bulnes, Macizos Central y Oriental* (in Spanish). Available from Llibreria Quera.

From Tuiza de Arriba to the Refugio de Casa Mieres. A walk through high meadows with glorious views of the rocky crags of the Macizo de Peña Ubiña. Several optional walks are possible to the summits of 2,417-meter Penã Ubiña and nearby peaks. **Walking Time:** 1 day. **Difficulty:** Moderately difficult. **Path Markings:** None.

Maps:
* Instituto Geográfico Nacional Mapa Topográfico 1:50,000, sheets 77 *La Plaza*, 78 *Pola de Lena* and 102 *Los Barrios de Luna.*

Path Description:
* *Bergwelt Spaniens* (in German). Available from GEO CENTER.

Montañas Gallegas

Galicia, in the northwestern corner of Spain, is a region of low wooded hills and green valleys. With the greatest rainfall of any region in Spain, it is a land of numerous rivers and streams, which empty into deep, almost fjord-like estuaries extending inland from the Atlantic Ocean to the west and the Cantabrian Sea to the north. The hills of the interior are technically part of the Cordillera Cantábrica, but lack the grandeur and stature of the great ranges to the east. Instead, they offer pleasant, easy rambles on lonely lanes and tracks through woodlands of pine and oak, alongside streams and lakes, and over open, rolling ridges of grass and scrub.

For those who prefer more rugged terrain, there is the Sierra y Picos de Ancares running north-south along the border of Lugo and León provinces, the westernmost of the high ridges of the Cordillera Cantábrica. Here, the highest peaks approach 2,000 meters in elevation and woodland gives way on the upper slopes to rocky crags draped with snow and open ridges covered by low, windswept heather and broom. In the high pastures are *pallozas*, primitive shepherds' huts with stone walls and peaked roofs of thatch.

Numerous walks are possible into the highlands, most on unmarked paths and game trails which lead past quaint villages nestling among fields and fruit orchards on the range's lower slopes. Although there are some rocky cliffs suitable for climbing, most of the peaks require only easy scrambles to reach their summits. And there are fine ridge walks with sweeping views in all directions.

The mountains are crossed by only one road and have been set aside as the Parque Nacional de Ancares. This reserve protects a wide variety of wildlife, including capercaillie, roe deer, hart, fallow deer, wild boar, chamois, wolves, martens and an occasional Pyrenean bear.

Lodgings are available throughout Galicia. Information on mountain huts, such as the albergue operated by the Club Ancares at Campa de Fieró, on the west side of the Sierra y Picos de Ancares, can be obtained from the Federación Gallega de Montañismo. Lists of other lodgings in and near the mountains are available upon request from each of the provincial tourist associations.

Useful Addresses

Federación Gallega de Montañismo (see *Address Directory*). Oversees mountaineering activities throughout the Montañas Galaicas. Can provide information on walking, climbing, ski mountaineering and cave exploration as well as a list of mountain refuges and schedules of walking and climbing tours, mountaineering courses and other activities organized by the federation and its affiliated clubs. Affiliated with 19 local mountaineering clubs. Staff speaks Gallego and Spanish.

The following tourist offices can provide general information on their respective provinces, including lodging lists, road maps and brochures describing features of interest. For their addresses and telephone numbers, see the *Address Directory*.

La Coruña: Oficina de Información y Turismo, La Coruña. Staff speaks Spanish and Portuguese.

Lugo: Oficina de Información y Turismo, Lugo. Staff speaks Spanish. Useful publications include:

• *Sierra de Ancares* (in English). A color brochure describing the range, with sections on game and fishing; walking, climbing and skiing; and accommodation and food. Gives the addresses and telephone numbers of local tourist offices. Also includes a color-shaded relief map and color photographs.

Orense: Oficina de Información y Turismo, Orense. Staff speaks Spanish.

Pontevedra: Oficina de Información y Turismo, Pontevedra. Staff speaks Spanish.

Maps

Galicia, including the Sierra y Picos de Ancares, is covered by the following topographical maps:

La Coruña Province: Instituto Geográfico Nacional Mapa Topográfico 1:50,000, sheets 1, 2, 6, 7, 8, 21, 22, 23, 43, 44, 45, 46, 67, 68, 69, 70, 71, 92, 93, 94, 95, 96, 119, 120, 121 and 151.

Orense Province: Instituto Geográfico Nacional Mapa Topográfico 1:50,000, sheets 186, 187, 188, 189, 190, 191, 224, 225, 226, 227, 228, 229, 263, 264, 265, 266, 301, 302, 303, 304 and 336.

Pontevedra Province: Instituto Geográfico Nacional Mapa Topográfico 1:50,000, sheets 121, 122, 152, 153, 154, 184, 185, 186, 222, 223, 224, 260, 261, 262, 298 and 299.

Lugo Province (including the Sierra y Picos de Ancares): Instituto Geográfico Nacional Mapa Topográfico 1:50,000, sheets 2, 3, 8, 9, 10, 23, 24, 25, 46, 47, 48, 49, 71, 72, 73, 74, 96, 97, 98, 99, 100, 122, 123, 124, 125, 154, 155, 156, 157, 188, 189, and 190.

Sierra y Picos de Ancares: Instituto Geográfico Nacional Mapa Topográfico 1:50,000, sheets 99, 100, 125, 126 and 157.

Guidebooks

- *Cumbres de Galicia: Monte Alba* (in Spanish). The first in a series of guides devoted to the mountains of Galicia. Available from the Club Montañeros Celtas (see *Address Directory*).

A list of other guidebooks, map-guides and *fichas* (or leaflets) which may have been published recently can be obtained from the Club Montañeros Celtas and the Federación Gallega de Montañismo (see *Address Directory*).

The Pyrenees

In a country richly blessed with high, rugged mountain ranges, the Pyrenees stand in a class by themselves. They are, in fact, one of the largest and grandest single mountain ranges in Europe. Unlike the Alps, which are a vast mountain system composed of numerous separate ranges, the Pyrenees are a single mountain mass of awesome proportions. They stretch east-west along the border of France and Spain for a distance of 435 kilometers (270 miles) and vary in width from 50 to 190 kilometers (30 to 120 miles). In the central part of the range, numerous peaks rise above 3,000 meters (9,840 feet), the highest being Pico de Aneto (3,424 meters; 11,233 feet). The greater part of the Pyrenees, as well as the highest peaks, lies in Spain.

Footpaths wind throughout the range, and innumerable routes are possible. You can wander through fertile valleys beneath snowy crags, stopping at quaint mountain villages clustered among orchards, fields and verdant pastures. Other paths lead into the heart of the mountains, through forests of beech, pine and silver fir; along leaping torrents in rocky gorges; to high basins above timberline where myriads of lakes are strewn among meadow and rock; and over high, rugged passes shouldered by mighty peaks. The experienced cross-country walker has a seemingly endless choice of routes. And for the climber there are challenging peaks on every horizon.

Although many of the paths are unmarked, numerous walking guides and maps—both in Spanish and French—exist to help walkers find their way. The Pyrenees, in fact, are the only mountains in Spain adequately covered by walking guides.

Lodgings are also less of a problem. Numerous mountain huts and refuges, including three national paradores, are scattered throughout the Pyrenees. Accommodation is also available in many of the towns and villages located in and around the mountains. During the winter, lodgings are available at the many ski resorts found in all parts of the range. A variety of cross-country routes—virtually all unmarked—radiate from these centers.

The Spanish Pyrenees consist of three districts: the Navarrese Pyrenees in the west; the Aragonese Pyrenees, which comprise the central portion of the range; and the Catalan Pyrenees to the east.

The Navarrese Pyrenees are lower and gentler in contour than those of Aragon and Catalunya. Here, footpaths lead through green meadows, beech woods, forests and delightful pastoral settings. Many peaks require only easy scrambles to reach their summits. Among the more popular walking areas are the pass of Ibañeta (or Roncesvalles) and the mountains surrounding the village of Irati, to the east of Roncesvalles.

The Aragonese Pyrenees comprise the highest, most rugged district, offering typically Alpine scenery, with snowy crags, high, lake-spangled basins, extensive meadows, awesome rock walls and deep, glacier-carved valleys. Of particular interest to walkers is the wild and beautiful Parque Nacional de Ordesa, where a high, lush valley alive with the music of cascades lies beneath a panoply of lofty peaks, including Monte Perdido (3,355 meters; 11,007 feet). Another excellent walking district surrounds the valley of Benasque, the steepest-walled canyon in the Pyrenees. Here, footpaths wind among the highest peaks in the range, including 3,424-meter Pico de Aneto on one side of the valley and 3,375-meter Pico de Poset on the other.

Also of special interest is the Sierra de Guara, a fantastic badlands in the foothills of the Aragonese Pyrenees. Here, you can follow tracks through a maze of cliffs, gorges and spectacular water-sculpted rock formations, stopping here and there to visit a remote village or bathe in a warm pool on a shady canyon floor.

The Catalan Pyrenees comprise the largest of the three districts. And if the peaks are not as high as those of Aragon, they are scarcely less rugged and no less equal in grandeur. Among the most beautiful places in the district is the Parque Nacional Aigües Tortes—Lago San Mauricio, where dozens of lakes reflect woods of pine and birch and rank upon rank of lofty crags. Nearby is the beautiful glacier-carved Vall d'Aran, from which numerous footpaths lead into the surrounding mountains. The peaks in the district are sheer and imposing, offering numerous challenging routes for the climber. Below the rugged crests lie high meadows and hundreds of lakes.

Further walking possibilities exist both in the Pyrenees of Andorra and France. You can also follow a portion of European Long-Distance Footpath E-4 (described in *On Foot Through Europe: A Trail Guide to Europe's Long-Distance Footpaths*), which enters Spain from France at Puigcerdà and strikes southward through Catalunya to the northern edge of Valencia province.

Useful Addresses

The following mountaineering federations can provide information on walking, climbing, ski mountaineering and cave exploration. They can also provide lists of their publications, information on the locations of mountain refuges, and schedules of the walking and climbing tours, mountaineering courses and other activities which they and their affiliated local clubs organize. Before writing the clubs, however, it is advisable to read the section on *Where to Get Walking Information* to ensure a better chance of a response.

See *Address Directory:*

Federación Aragonesa de Montañismo. Can provide information on the Aragonese Pyrenees. Affiliated with 30 local clubs devoted to mountaineering and cave exploration. Staff speaks Spanish.

Federación Catalana de Montañismo. Can provide information on the Catalan Pyrenees. Affiliated with 145 local clubs devoted to mountaineering, skiing and other activities. Staff speaks Catalan and Spanish.

Federación Vasco-Navarra de Montañismo. Can provide information on the Navarrese Pyrenees. Affiliated with 145 local clubs devoted to mountaineering and other activities. Staff speaks Euskara and Spanish.

The following tourist offices can provide general information on their respective provinces, including lodging lists, road maps and brochures describing features of interest.

See *Address Directory:*

Barcelona: Oficina de Información de Turismo, Barcelona. Staff speaks Catalan, Spanish, French and some English.

Girona (Gerona): Oficina de Información de Turismo, Girona. Staff speaks Catalan, Spanish, French and some English.

Guipuzcoa: Oficina de Información de Turismo, San Sebastián. Staff speaks Spanish and French.

Lérida: Oficina de Información de Turismo, Lérida. Staff speaks Catalan and Spanish.

Huesca: Oficina de Información de Turismo, Huesca. Staff speaks Spanish.

Navarra: Oficina de Información de Turismo, Pamplona. Staff speaks Spanish.

Zaragoza: Oficina de Información de Turismo, Zaragoza. Staff speaks Spanish.

All of these offices can provide the following tourist brochure about the Pyrenees:

- *The Pyrenees, Spain* (in English). A useful introduction to the Pyrenees with numerous color photographs and a road map showing the locations (and altitudes) of major peaks and the national parks. Describes the three major districts of the Pyrenees, as well as their principal towns and villages, refuges and hotels, monasteries, spas, cuisine and local festivals and folklore. Includes a list of winter resorts and gives the addresses and telephone numbers of local tourist offices. Does not describe walks or walking areas, but is useful for an overall view of the Pyrenees. Free on request.

Maps

The Pyrenees are covered by the following topographical maps:

Aragonese Pyrenees (Pirineos Centrales): Instituto Geográfico Nacional Mapa Topográfico 1:50,000, sheets 118, 144, 145, 146, 147, 148, 175, 176, 177, 178, 179, 180, 207, 208, 209, 210, 211, 212, 213, 246, 247, 248, 249, 250, 251, 286, 287, 288 and 289.

Catalan Pyrenees (Pirineos Orientales): Instituto Geográfico Nacional Mapa Topográfico 1:50,000, sheets 118 bis., 148, 149, 150, 180, 181, 182, 183 (covers part of Andorra), 213, 214, 215, 216, 217, 218, 219, 220, 251, 252, 253, 254, 255, 256, 257, 258, 289, 290, 291, 293, 294, 295 and 296.

Navarrese Pyrenees (Pirineos Occidentales): Instituto Geográfico Nacional Mapa Topográfico 1:50,000, sheets 64, 65, 66, 89, 90, 91, 91 bis., 114, 115, 116, 117, 118, 140, 141, 142, 143, 144, 172, 173, 174 and 175.

Guidebooks & Map-Guides

For details on the guidebooks and map-guides covering the Pyrenees, see the sections on *Maps* and *Guidebooks* earlier in this chapter. In addition to the guidebooks listed for the Pyrenees, the following is also useful:

* *Bergwelt Spaniens* (in German) by Agustin Jolis, Fink-Kümmerly + Frey, Stuttgart, 1973. Describes 44 walks in the Pyrenees. Available from GEO CENTER.

A price list, as well as a list of other guidebooks, map-guides and *chas* (or leaflets) covering the footpaths in the Pyrenees can be obtained upon request from Llibreria Quera.

Suggested Walks

From Orbaiceta to the headwaters of the Río Urtxuria and return. A circuit through the heart of the Navarran Pyrenees east of Roncesvalles. Follows the high, grassy ridge top of the Sierra de Abodi (magnificent views in all directions in clear weather) to the headwaters of the Río Urtxuria, beneath 2,018-meter (6,619-foot) Pico d'Ory, the third highest peak in the district. Return is by way of the Urtxuria Valley, with its tumbling waters, open meadows and lovely fir forests. About half the route is easy cross-country rambling. **Walking Time:** 10 hours; best done in two days, with time for side trips. **Difficulty:** Easy to moderately difficult. **Path Markings:** Yellow arrows on the track in lower Urtxuria Valley; otherwise none.
Maps:
* Instituto Geográfico Nacional Mapa Topográfico 1:50,000, sheets 91 *Valcarlos*, 91 bis *Mendi-zar*, 116 *Garralda* and 117 *Ochagavía*.
Path Description:
* *Rutas Montañeras I, Ory—Velate* (in Spanish). Available from Llibreria Quera.

From Torla to Monte Perdido. Through the lush Ordesa Valley in the Parque Nacional de Ordesa, with its magnificent stands of silver and black pine, beech, juniper, silver fir, poplar, hazel, birch, oak, ash, yew, linden and rhododendron. Past the lovely Arazas cascades, with a final climb to Lago Helado and the summit of Monte Perdido, highest peak in the region. Superlative mountain scenery from start to finish. **Walking Time:** 9½ hours (one way). **Difficulty:** Easy to moderately difficult. **Path Markings:** None.

Maps:
• Instituto Geográfico Nacional Mapa Topográfico 1:50,000, sheets 146 *Bujaruelo* and 178 *Broto.*

Path Description:
• *Bergwelt Spaniens* (in German). Available from GEO CENTER.

From Espot to Arties: A supreme mountain tour through the Catalan Pyrenees, by way of San Mauricio Lake, Ratera Pass, the great lake of Colomers, Colomers Pass, the Refugio de Ventosa y Calvell, Güellacrestada Pass and the Refugio de la Restanca. The route crosses three passes in excess of 2,000 meters elevation and winds past more than two dozen lakes, including San Mauricio in the Parque Nacional de Aigües Tortes-San Mauricio. Great forests, broad meadows and dozens of peaks approaching 3,000 meters elevation. Breathtaking scenery from start to finish. **Walking Time:** 2 to 3 days. **Difficulty:** Moderately difficult to difficult. **Path markings:** A few cairns; otherwise, none.

Maps:
• Instituto Geográfico Nacional Mapa Topográfico 1:50,000, sheets 149 *Isil* and 181 *Esterri de Aneu.*

Path Description:
• *Pallars-Aran* (in Spanish). From the *Colección de Guias del Centre Excursionista de Catalunya.* See description of entire series, in the section on *Guidebooks.*

Sistema Central: the Sierras de Gredos & Guadarrama

The Sistema Central—or Central Mountain System—rises a few kilometers to the northwest of Madrid, running in a northeast-southwest direction across Spain's great central plateau—the Meseta—for a distance of some 300 kilometers (185 miles). It divides the watersheds of the two great rivers of Castile: the Río Duero in the north and the Río Tajo in the south.

The Sistema Central largely consists of two separate mountain blocks. On the west is the Sierra de Gredos, a great uplifted granite block stretching some 150 kilometers between Bejar and Avila. To the east is the somewhat lower, less rugged Sierra de Guadarrama. Separating the two ranges is the gentle upland of the Paramera de Avila—the Avila Moor. From the moor, the Sierra de Guadarrama extends northeastward for nearly 100 kilometers to Somosierra Pass. East of this pass rises the Sierra de Ayllon and the Somosierra, minor ranges that merge imperceptibly with the mountains of the Sistema Ibérico in Soria province.

Numerous walks are possible throughout the Sistema Central, some on gentle forest tracks meandering through the pines, others along narrow footpaths wandering among the maze of crests and gorges. You can also strike off cross-country through high open meadows and along barren granite ridges overlooking lake basins hemmed in by a wilderness of jagged crests.

About 25 kilometers of footpaths have been completely marked with red or, in most cases, yellow circles and signs indicating distances to various destinations. Another 40 to 50 kilometers are marked by circles but lack the distance indicators. Finally, some 250 kilometers are marked by cairns. In addition, there are numerous unmarked paths, most of which are easy to follow with the appropriate 1:50,000 topographical maps. Local villagers can also help you find your way.

The Sierra de Gredos is the wilder of the two ranges and features the most spectacular mountain scenery. Ridges crowned by arrays of pinnacles drop steeply to narrow gorges and boulder-strewn lake basins. Of particular interest to walkers are the Circo de Gredos, where the rugged heights of 2,592-meter Almanzor, the highest peak in the Sistema Central, are mirrored in the cold, serene waters of a mountain lake; and the nearby gorge of the Cinco Lagunas, five gem-like tarns nestled in settings of polished granite. Other fine walking areas include La Mira peak and Los Galayos, the Gredos and Rio Tormes national preserves, the Sierra de la Nava, and in the extreme west, the Sierra de Bejar.

At lower elevations you can walk through pine forests and fruit orchards, stopping at country villages or visiting the many historical monuments in the region. These include beautifully preserved medieval castles, walled towns—notably Avila—and the historic Venta Juradera—the Inn of the Oath—where Isabella was proclaimed Queen of Castile.

The contours of the Sierra de Guadarrama tend to be somewhat gentler than those of Gredos, yet there are notable exceptions, such as La Pedriza de Manzanares, whose crags are a favorite objective for climbers. Other areas of interest to walkers are the Valle de la Acebada, with its beautiful pine forest and tumbling streams; the rugged crest of La Mujer Muerta, which can be walked from end to end (see "Suggested Walks" below); and the Macizo de Peñalera (2,430 meters; 7,972 feet), the highest, most majestic peak in the range, where the waters of the beautiful Laguna Grande lie beneath steep precipices and great ravines.

Numerous ski tours are possible in both the Gredos and Guadarrama, as well as in the Sierra de Ayllon, where 2,273-meter Pico del Lobo can be reached from the nearby La Panilla ski resort. The same peak can be easily attained by walkers during the summer.

Several mountain huts are scattered throughout the Sistema Central, and there is a national parador not far from the Circo de Gredos peaks. Accommodation is also easily obtained in the surrounding towns. You can even stay in Madrid—a mere 70 kilometers to the south of Guadarrama—travel to the range by train, take a walk and return by train to Madrid—all in one day. The Sierra de Gredos is similarly accessible by bus from Avila.

Useful Addresses

See *Address Directory:*

Federación Castellana de Montañismo. Can provide information on walking, climbing, ski mountaineering and cave exploration throughout the Sistema Central. Can also provide a list of its publications, information on the location of mountain refuges, and schedules of the walking and climbing tours, mountaineering courses and other activities organized by the federation and its affiliated clubs. Affiliated with 153 local clubs devoted to mountaineering, cave exploration and other activities. Staff speaks Spanish. A few staff members also speak some French and English.

Federación Española de Montañismo, F.E.M. Oversees mountaineering activities throughout Spain. Publishes several guidebooks and maps to the Sistema Central. Also owns and operates several refuges in the Sierra de Gredos and Sierra de Guadarrama. Can provide information on mountain guides, as well as on walking and climbing tours, mountaineering courses and other activities organized by the F.E.M. and its national committees. Staff speaks Spanish and French.

The following tourist offices can provide general information on their respective provinces, including lodging lists, road maps and brochures describing features of interest.

See *Address Directory:*

Avila: Oficina de Información de Turismo, Avila. Staff speaks Spanish. Useful publications include:

- *Sierra de Gredos* (in English). A brochure describing the range and suggesting several walks. Includes a color-shaded relief map and numerous color photographs. Provides the addresses and telephone numbers of the provincial tourist delegation, the tourist information office in Avila, the Spanish Skiing Federation and the F.E.M.

Madrid: Oficina de Información de Turismo, Madrid. Staff speaks Spanish, French and English. Among the useful publications available from the office is:

- *Sierra de Guadarrama* (in English). A brochure describing the range and indicating some walks and ski tours. Also lists and describes inns and shelters, provides technical data on the lifts and tows at the ski resort of Puerto de Navacerrada and briefly describes towns and historical attractions. Includes a color-shaded relief map and numerous color photographs. Gives the addresses and telephone numbers of local walking and skiing clubs.

Segovia: Oficina de Información de Turismo, Segovia. Can also provide the brochure *Sierra de Guadarrama* described above. Staff speaks Spanish.

Maps

The Sistema Central is covered by the following topographical maps:

Sierra de Gredos: Instituto Geográfico Nacional Mapa Topográfico 1:50,000, sheets 529, 530, 531, 553, 554, 555, 556, 576, 577, 578 and 579.

Sierra de Guadarrama: Instituto Geográfico Nacional Mapa Topográfico, special map sheet: *Sierra de Guadarrama*. Consists of sheets 483, 484, 508, and 590. Co-published by the F.E.M.

Paramera de Avila & Sierra del Malagon: Instituto Geográfico Nacional Mapa Topográfico 1:50,000, sheets, 507, 532, 533 and 557.

Sierra de Ayllon & Somosierra: Instituto Geográfico Nacional Mapa Topográfico 1:50,000, sheets 405, 432, 433, 458, 459 and 485.

Guidebooks & Map-Guides

For details on the guidebooks and map-guides covering the Sistema Central, see the sections on *Maps* and *Guidebooks* earlier in this chapter. In addition to the guidebooks listed for the Sistema Central, *Bergwelt Spaniens*, published in German by Fink-Kümmerly + Frey, describes 10 walks in the Sierra de Gredos and Sierra de Guadarrama.

A list of other guidebooks, map-guides and *fichas* covering the Sistema Central can be obtained from the F.E.M. and the Federación Castellana de Montañismo, as well as from Llibreria Quera.

Suggested Walks

From La Plataforma to Cinco Lagunas. Spectacular, rugged mountain scenery, with jagged peaks, rock walls, boulder fields and beautiful mountain lakes. The route visits the Circo de Gredos Lake and refuge enroute to the Cinco Lagunas. Possible side trips include scrambles to the high cols of Almanzor and La Galana. **Walking Time:** 4 hours. **Difficulty:** Easy to moderately difficult. **Path Markings:** Cairns.
Maps:
• Instituto Geográfico Nacional Mapa Topográfico 1:50,000, sheet 577 *Bohoyo*.
Path Description:
• *Bergwelt Spaniens* (in German). Available from GEO CENTER.

From Cercedilla to Estación de el Espinar. The classic ridge walk in the Sierra de Guadarrama, leading from summit to summit along the top of the massif of La Mujer Muerta. Spectacular views of the nearby mountains and more distant lowlands. Visits five major summits enroute, including 2,193-meter (7,195-foot) Pinaraja. **Walking Time:** 9 hours. **Difficulty:** Moderately difficult. **Path Markings:** None; mostly cross-country.
Special Note: An attractive feature of this walk is that it begins and ends at separate train stations on the line between Segovia and Madrid.
Maps:
• Institute Geográfico Nacional Mapa Topográfico 1:50,000, sheets 507 *El Espinar* and 508 *Cercedilla*.
Path Description:
• *Alta Ruta*, April 1977, No. 1, pages 16 and 17. This is the journal of the Club Alpino Maliciosa. You may be able to obtain or inspect this particular issue by visiting the club office (see *Address Directory*).

Sistema Ibérico

The Sistema Ibérico is a broad, irregular mountain system angling southeastward across Spain from the provinces of Burgos and Logroño in the north to Valencia in the south, a distance of some 400 kilometers (250 miles). At its broadest, in the provinces of Teruel and Cuenca, the mountain system forms a convoluted upland roughly 200 kilometers (125 miles) across.

The highest ranges in the system, with numerous peaks topping 2,000 meters elevation, are located in the provinces of Burgos, Logrono and Soria. These include the Sierra de Moncayo, Sierra de Cameros and the Picos del Urbión, whose bare, rugged crests rise steeply above forests of beech and pine. Nestled among the forests are numerous picturesque mountain villages which provide good starting points for walks into the mountains.

South of Soria the mountains fall away to a succession of lower ranges crossed by the Madrid-Zaragoza highway. Beyond the highway, elevations begin to increase again to form the broad, rugged upland surrounding the city of Teruel. To the west of the city rises the Sierra de Albarracin, with deep, rocky gorges, meadows, vast pine forests, mineral springs, caves with prehistoric drawings and numerous peaks approaching 2,000 meters elevation. Beyond the Sierra de Albarracin stretches the *Serrania*—mountain district—of Cuenca province, with its pine forests, fantastic rock formations, cascades and streams. From the heights above Cuenca is a westward sweeping view out over the great flat plain of La Mancha, where Don Quixote tilted windmills in his quest for the chivalric ideal.

East of the Teruel lies the rugged upland known as the Maestrazgo, which extends into the province of Castellón. Although this mountain region has only one peak higher than 2,000 meters—2,024-meter Peñarroya—it is characterized by extremely rugged ridges and rocky chasms. The region also has lush, green valleys, picturesque villages, forests of pine and oak, and mountain torrents broken by cascades and waterfalls. From Cervera Castle in the province of Castellón you can see the shimmering Mediterranean to the east and the hills of Tarragona to the north.

The Sistema Ibérico is perhaps the least developed mountain region in

Spain for walking. No guidebooks exist to the region and the paths throughout are unmarked. The best way to plan walks in the region is to obtain one or more of the map-guides mentioned below and then consult local walking clubs or villagers for precise directions. The advantages of walking in the Sistema Ibérico include not only the splendid wild scenery, but a solitude perhaps unequaled in any of the other Spanish ranges.

Useful Addresses

The following mountaineering federations can provide information on walking, climbing, ski mountaineering and cave exploration in their respective provinces. They can also provide lists of their publications, information on the location of mountain refuges, and schedules of the walking and climbing tours, mountaineering courses and other activities which they and their affiliated local clubs organize. Before writing the clubs, however, it is advisable to read the section on *Where to Get Walking Information* to ensure a better chance of a response.

See *Address Directory:*

Federación Aragonesa de Montañismo. Oversees mountaineering activities in the provinces of Huesca, Teruel and Zaragoza. Affiliated with 30 local clubs devoted to mountaineering, cave exploration and other activities. Staff speaks Spanish.

Federación Castellana de Montañismo. Oversees mountaineering activities in, among others, the provinces of Burgos, Logroño, Cuenca, Guadalajara and Soria. Affiliated with 153 local clubs devoted to mountaineering, cave exploration and other activities. Staff speaks Spanish.

Federación Valenciana de Montañismo. Oversees mountaineering activities in the provinces of Albacete, Alicante, Castellón, Murcia and Valencia. Affiliated with 41 local clubs devoted to mountaineering, cave exploration and other activities. Staff speaks Catalan and Spanish.

The following tourist offices can provide general information on their respective provinces, including lodging lists, road maps and brochures describing features of interest.

See *Address Directory:*

Burgos: Oficina de Información de Turismo, Burgos. Staff speaks Spanish.

Castellón: Oficina de Información de Turismo, Castellón de la Plana. Staff speaks Spanish. Useful publications include:

• *El Maestrazgo* (in English). A brochure describing this mountain region, including its scenery, history, towns and villages, and local customs and cuisine. Includes a color-shaded relief map and numerous color photographs.

Cuenca: Oficina de Información de Turismo, Cuenca. Staff speaks Spanish.

Guadalajara: Oficina de Información de Turismo, Guadalajara. Staff speaks Spanish.

Logroño: Oficina de Información de Turismo, Logroño. Staff speaks Spanish.

Soria: Oficina de Información de Turismo, Soria. Staff Speaks Spanish.

Teruel: Oficina de Información de Turismo, Teruel. Can also provide the publication *El Maestrazgo* (described above). Staff speaks Spanish.

Valencia: Oficina de Información de Turismo, Valencia. Staff speaks Spanish.

Zaragoza: Oficina de Información de Turismo, Zaragoza. Staff speaks Spanish.

Maps

The Sistema Ibérico is covered by the following topographical maps:

Burgos: Instituto Geográfico Nacional Mapa Topográfico 1:50,000, sheets 201, 202, 239, 240, 277, 278, 315 and 316.

Castellón: Instituto Geográfico Nacional Mapa Topográfico 1:50,000, sheets 519, 520, 544, 545, 569, 570, 592, 593, 614, 615, 639, 640 and 667.

Cuenca: Instituto Geográfico Nacional Mapa Topográfico 1:50,000, sheets 538, 539, 563, 564, 587, 588, 610, 611, 612, 636, 637, 638, 664 and 665.

Guadalajara: Instituto Geográfico Nacional Mapa Topográfico 1:50,000, sheets 461, 462, 463, 464, 487, 488, 489, 490, 512, 513, 514, 515, 538, 539, 540 and 565.

Logroño: Instituto Geográfico Nacional Mapa Topográfico 1:50,000, sheets 202, 203, 204, 239, 240, 241, 242, 243, 278, 279, 280, 281 and 319.

Soria: Instituto Geográfico Nacional Mapa Topográfico 1:50,000, sheets 316, 317, 318, 319, 349, 350, 351, 352, 378, 379, 380, 406, 407, 408, 434, 435, 436, 462 and 463.

Tervel: Instituto Geográfico Nacional Mapa Topográfico 1:50,000, sheets 465, 466, 467, 490, 491, 492, 493, 494, 515, 516, 517, 518, 519, 520, 540, 541, 542, 543, 544, 565, 566, 567, 568, 569, 588, 589, 590, 591, 592, 612, 613, 614, 638 and 639.

Valencia: Instituto Geográfico Nacional Mapa Topográfico 1:50,000, sheets 638, 639, 665, 666 and 667.

Zaragoza: Instituto Geográfico Nacional Mapa Topográfico 1:50,000, sheets 320, 352, 380, 381, 408, 409, 436, 437, 463, 464, 465, 490 and 491.

Map-Guides

- *Mapas-Guías de Macizos Montañosos Españoles* (in Spanish). Seven titles cover various parts of the Sistema Ibérico. See description of series, and list of titles for the Sistema Ibérico in the section on *Maps*.

A list of other guidebooks, map-guides and *fichas* which may have been published recently to the Sistema Ibérico can be obtained on request from Llibreria Quera.

Suggested Walks

Walks are possible throughout the Sistema Ibérico. Of particular interest to walkers, however, are the following areas: Laguna Negra and Urbión, in the Picos del Urbión; the mountains around Hoyos de Iregua, in the Sierra de Cameros; the Oncala Pass area, in the Sierra de Moncayo; the headwaters of the Río Tajo, in the Sierra de Albarracin; the Ciudad Encantada in the Serrania of Cuenca province; and the Peñarroya district of the Maestrazgo.

Sistema Penibético & the Sierra Nevada

High above the city of Granada and the magnificent Moorish palace of the Alhambra rise the lofty summits of the Sierra Nevada, the highest mountain range in the Iberian Peninsula. Iberia's two highest peaks—Mulhacen (3,481 meters; 11, 420 feet) and Veleta (3,428 meters; 11, 246 feet) are located in the western end of the range, along with nearly two dozen other summits above 3,000 meters elevation. From this crown of peaks, the Sierra Nevada extends eastward for about 110 kilometers (68 miles), running parallel to the Costa del Sol and rising only a few kilometers inland from the sea.

Numerous footpaths lead into the highest reaches of the range through rocky gorges, along gentle, open ridge tops, and past high lake basins nestled beneath the peaks. You can also wander for days along the high backbone of the range, from which the views are spectacular in all directions, but especially to the south, where the Mediterranean forms a serene blue plain stretching toward Africa. Despite its high altitude and crown of rugged peaks, the summit crest is surprisingly gentle, dropping away abruptly on one side, but sloping gently downslope on the other.

One national parador and several mountain huts provide accommodation in the Sierra Nevada. Near Las Sietes Lagunas, a series of several tarns on the eastern side of Mulhacen, a natural refuge exists beneath a great pile of giant boulders. Lodgings are also available in Granada, which provides quick access to the highest parts of the range, as well as in several other towns strung along the base of the mountains.

Sierra Nevada means the "snowy range," a fitting name from November until June, when the upper slopes are mantled in white. Because of the gentle terrain on the summit ridge, the opportunities for cross-country skiing are excellent. And since the range is the southernmost in Europe, it enjoys numerous sunny days even in midwinter.

The Sierra Nevada is the major range in the Sistema Penibético, the longest in Spain, stretching from the Río Jucar, in the province of Albacete, to the straits of Gibraltar—a distance of some 480 kilometers (300 miles).

The chain is divided by a fault zone into several northern and southern ranges. The Sierra Nevada is the principal southern range. Preeminent among the northern ranges is the Sierra de Cazorla, in the province of

Jaen. Although the highest peaks in this range barely rise above 2,000 meters, the mountains are extremely rugged, with rocky crags and deep gorges. The headwaters of the Río Guadalquivir, the largest river in southern Spain, rise high in the eastern part of the range, tumbling in cascades and waterfalls down narrow, rocky gorges to a broad valley bordered by peaks.

Numerous footpaths crisscross the Sierra de Cazorla, winding through woodlands of evergreen oak, English oak, poplar and arbutus, and through forests of pine and juniper. You can climb slopes fragrant with such aromatic plants as rosemary, thyme, lavender, sweet marjoram and origanum, or follow narrow gorges with tumbling streams to high, barren crests where ibex and moufflon sheep scramble among the precipitous rocks. The Sierra de Cazorla is noted not only for its scenery, but for the abundance and variety of its flora and fauna, which include several species found nowhere else.

There are a fair number of refuges and forest huts scattered throughout the mountains. Accommodation is also available in some of the towns at the base of the range. Moreover, the city of Jaen is located only a few kilometers to the west.

In addition to the Sierra Nevada and the Sierra de Cazorla, there are several other ranges of interest to walkers in the Sistema Penebético. These include the Segura de la Sierra, east of the Sierra de Cazorla; the Sierras de Juelma, Noalejo and Valdepeñas, south of Jaen; the Sierra de los Filabres, in the province of Almeria; and the Sierra de Almijara, in the province of Malaga.

Useful Addresses

See *Address Directory:*

Federación Andaluza de Montañismo. Oversees mountaineering activities throughout Andalusia, which encompasses most of the Sistema Penibético and the Sierra Nevada. Can provide information on walking, climbing, ski mountaineering and cave exploration, as well as a list of mountain refuges and schedules of walking and climbing tours, mountaineering courses and other activities organized by the federation and its affiliated clubs. Affiliated with 62 local clubs devoted to mountaineering and cave exploration. Staff speaks English and Spanish.

Federación Valenciana de Montañismo. Oversees mountaineering activities in the Segura de la Sierra and the portion of the Sierra de Cazorla which extends into the province of Albacete. Affiliated with one local club devoted to cave exploration in Albacete. Staff speaks English and Spanish.

The following tourist information offices can provide general information on their respective provinces, including lodging lists, road maps and brochures describing features of interest.

See *Address Directory:*

Albacete: Oficina de Información de Turismo, Albacete. Staff speaks Spanish.

Alicante: Oficina de Información de Turismo, Alicante. Staff speaks Spanish and English.

Almería: Oficina de Información de Turismo, Almería. Staff speaks Spanish. Useful publications include:

• *Sierra Nevada* (in English). A brochure describing the range, with special sections on climate, skiing, hunting and fishing, and local villages. Lists hotels and shelters and gives the addresses and phone numbers of local tourist offices and walking clubs. Includes a color-shaded relief map and numerous color photographs.

Granada: Oficina de Información de Turismo, Granada. Can also provide the publication *Sierra Nevada* (described above). Staff speaks Spanish.

Jaen: Oficina de Información de Turismo, Jaen. Staff speaks Spanish. Useful publications include:

• *Sierra de Cazorla* (in English). A brochure describing the range, with sections on scenery, villages, roads and tracks, flora and fauna, folklore and cuisine. Includes a color-shaded relief map showing wildlife areas and major footpaths. Numerous color photographs.

Malaga: Oficina de Información de Turismo, Malaga. Staff speaks Spanish and English.

Murcia: Oficina de Información de Turismo, Murcia. Staff speaks Spanish.

Maps

The Sistema Penibético is covered by the following topographical maps:

Albacete (including the Segura de la Sierra and part of the Sierra de Cazorla): Instituto Geográfico Nacional Mapa Topográfico 1:50,000, sheets 816, 817, 818, 819, 841, 842, 843, 844, 866, 867, 868, 869, 888, 889 and 909.

Alicante: Instituto Geográfico Nacional Mapa Topográfico 1:50,000, sheets 819, 820, 821, 845, 846, 847, 870, 871 and 872.

Almería (including the Sierra de los Filabres and part of the Sierra Nevada): Instituto Geográfico Nacional Mapa Topográfico 1:50,000, sheets 930, 931, 951, 952, 973, 974, 994, 995, 996, 1.012, 1.013, 1.014, 1.028, 1.029, 1.030, 1.043 and 1.044.

Granada (including part of the Sierra Nevada): Instituto Geográfico

Nacional Mapa Topográfico 1:50,000, sheets 908, 909, 929, 930, 949, 950, 951, 970, 971, 972, 973, 990, 991, 992, 993, 994, 995, 1.007, 1.008, 1.009, 1.010, 1.011, 1.012, 1.024, 1.025, 1.026, 1.027, 1.028, 1.040, 1.041, 1.042 and 1.043.

Jaen (including the Sierras de Juelma, Noalejo and Valdepenas and part of the Sierra de Cazorla): Instituto Geográfico Nacional Mapa Topográfico 1:50,000, sheets 886, 887, 888, 907, 908, 909, 926, 927, 928, 929, 946, 947, 948, 949, 950, 968, 969, 970, 971, 990 and 991.

Malaga (including the Sierra de Almijara): Instituto Geográfico Nacional Mapa Topográfico 1:50,000, sheets 1.006, 1.007, 1.022, 1.023, 1.024, 1.037, 1.038, 1.039, 1.040, 1.050, 1.051, 1.052, 1.063, 1.064 and 1.065.

Murcia (including part of the Segura de la Sierra): Instituto Geográfico Nacional Mapa Topográfico 1:50,000, sheets 818, 819, 844, 845, 868, 869, 870, 889, 890, 891, 892, 909, 910, 911, 930, 931, 932, 952, 953, 974 and 975.

Sierra Nevada: Instituto Geográfico Nacional Mapa Topográfico 1:50,000, sheets 1.010, 1.011, 1.012, 1.026, 1.027, 1.028, 1.029, 1.042, 1.043 and 1.044

Guidebooks & Map-Guides

For details on the guidebooks and map-guides covering the Sistema Penibético and the Sierra Nevada, see the sections on *Maps* and *Guidebooks* earlier in this chapter. A price list, as well as a list of other guidebooks, map-guides and *fichas* (or leaflets) covering the footpaths in the Sistema Penibético can be obtained upon request from Llibreria Quera and the Federación Andaluza Montañismo.

Suggested Walk

From Albergue Universitario to Siete Lagunas: A grand ridge walk in the Sierra Nevada passing five mountain lakes enroute and ending at a picturesque chain of seven lakes on the east slope of 3,481-meter Mulhacen. Walks are possible to the summits of Veleta and Mulhacen, the highest peaks on the Iberian Peninsula. Numerous side trips are also possible. Includes an overnight stay in the Refugio Natural, a boulder cave on the shore of Lago Hondera, one of the Siete Lagunas. **Walking Time:** 7 hours. **Difficulty:** Easy to moderately difficult. **Path Markings:** None.
Maps:
• Instituto Geográfico Nacional Mapa Topográfico 1:50,000, sheets 1.027 *Güéjar-Sierra* and 1.028 *Aldeire.*
Path Description:
• *Itinerarios del Macizo de Sierra Nevada,* Serie: *Recorridos de Alta Montaña,* Fichas 3 and 13 (in Spanish). See description under "Sistema Pentibético & the Sierra Nevada" in the section on *Guidebooks.* Available from walking clubs, bookstores and sport shops in Granada.

Address Directory

A

- *Arxiu Bibliogràfic de la Unió Excursionista de Catalunya,* Avenida José Antonio 580, Barcelona 11. Tel. (93) 254 32 47.

B

- *Baqueira Beret, S.A.,* Paseo de Grana 2, Barcelona 7. Tel. (93) 318 27 76 or 318 27 76.

C

- *Cantur,* Calle Juan de la Cosa 1, Santander. Tel. (942) 27 04 38. For information on snow conditions: Tel. (942) 75 10 99.
- *Cayetano Enriquez de Salamanca,* Apartado Correos 2413, Madrid.
- *Centro de Análisis y Predicción* (Ciudad Universitaria), Apartado 285, Madrid 3. Tel. (91) 244 35 00.
- *Cerler,* Calle Marco Aurelio 8, Barcelona 6. Tel. (93) 228 95 96. For information on snow conditions: Tel. (93) 228 95 56.
- *Certusa,* Plaza Isabel la Católica 1, Granada. Tel. (958) 48 03 00, 48 03 01 or 48 03 02. Permanent information number: Tel. (958) 22 75 00.
- *Club Alpino Español,* Mayor 6, Madrid 13. Tel. (91) 222 79 51.
- *Club Alpino Maliciosa,* Augusto Figueroa, 37-2°, Madrid 4. Tel. (91) 222 97 34.
- *Club Montañeros Celtas,* Marqués de Valladares 19, bajos, Vigo. Tel. (986) 21 76 08.
- *Comité Catalá de Senders de Gran Recorregut,* Rambles 61, Barcelona 2. Tel. (93) 302 64 16 or 302 22 84.

D

- *Delegación en Baleares,* Pedro Alcántara Peña 33, Palma de Mallorca. Tel. (971) 46 02 67.
- *Diez Deportes.* Four locations: Barcelo 7, Madrid 4, Tel. (91) 445 48 07; P.° de La Habana 5, Madrid 16, Tel. (91) 261 51 90; P.° de Extremadura 13, Madrid 13, Tel. (91) 464 28 88; and Bravo Murillo 177, Madrid 20, Tel. (91) 450 28 52.

- *Diputación Provincial de León,* Plaza de San Marcelo, León. Tel. (987) 23 35 00. For information on snow conditions: Tel. Puebla de Lillo (León) 39.
- *Diputación Provincial de Oviedo,* Plaza de Generalissimo, Oviedo. Tel. (985) 21 55 06. For information on snow conditions: Tel. (985) 21 55 06.

E

- *Editorial Alpina,* Apartado de Correos 3, Granollers.
- *Editorial Montblanc,* Apartado de Correos 3, Granollers.
- *Editorial SERPA,* Apartado Correos 35.167, Barcelona.
- *El Sherpa,* two locations: Hortaleza 52, Madrid 4, Tel. (91) 231 38 36 and Juan Duque 32, Madrid, Tel. (91) 266 78 66.
- *Emergency:* Call the *Guardia Civil* (consult the front pages of the telephone directory for the local number).
- *Ensija,* Berga (Barcelona). Tel. (93) 821 01 80.
- *Escuela Nacional de Alta Montaña,* D. Amadeo Botella, Calle Totena 8, Valencia 8. Tel. (96) 326 33 32.
- *Eskamp, S.L.,* Calle Hipólito Rovira 10, Valencia. Tel. (96) 365 95 58. For information on snow conditions: Tel. Alcala de la Selva 17.
- *Estación Alpina de Cotos,* Calle San Ramon Nonato 1, Madrid 16. Tel. (91) 215 59 39. Permanent information number: Tel. (91) 852 04 16. For information on runs and snow conditions: (recorded message) Tel. (91) 215 59 39.
- *Estación Invernal Valle de Astun, S.A.,* Avenida Independencia 19, Zaragoza. Tel. (976) 21 76 77 or 21 76 78.
- *Estación de Invierno (Miesa),* Calvo Sotelo 11, Manzaneda (Orense). Tel. (988) 21 46 04. For information on snow conditions: Tel. Puebla de Trives (Orense) 460.
- *Explotaciones Turisticas de Candanchu (Etuksa),* Candanchu (Huesca). Tel. (974) 37 31 92.

F

- *F.E.M.,* see *Federación Española de Montañismo.*
- *Federació d'Entitats Excursionistes de Catalunya* (Federación Catalana de Montañismo), Rambles 61, 1.°, Barcelona 2. Tel. (93) 302 64 16.
- *Federación Andaluza de Montañismo,* Avenida Reyes Católicos 1, 4., Granada.
- *Federación Aragonesa de Montañismo,* Albareda 7, 4.°, 4.ª, Zaragoza. Tel. (976) 22 79 71.

- *Federación Asturiana de Montañismo,* Melquíades Alvarez 16, Oviedo. Tel. (985) 21 10 99.
- *Federación Canaria de Montañismo,* La Naval 32, Las Palmas de Gran Canaria. No telephone.
- *Federación Cántabra de Montañismo,* Pablo Carnica 4, Torrelavega (Santander). Tel. (942) 89 06 90.
- *Federación Castellana de Montañismo,* Apodaca 16, Madrid 4. Tel. (91) 448 07 24.
- *Federación Catalana de Montañismo,* see *Federació d'Entitats Excursionistes de Catalunya.*
- *Federación Española de Montañismo (F.E.M.),* Alberto Aguilera 3, 4° izquierda, Madrid 15. Tel. (91) 445 13 82.
- *Federación Gallega de Montañismo,* Colón 9, pral., Vigo (Pontevedra). Tel. (986) 22 42 92.
- *Federación Leonesa de Montañismo,* Alcázar de Toledo 16 (Casa del Deporte), León. Tel. (987) 22 73 00.
- *Federación Palentina de Montañismo,* Onésimo Redondo 6, Palencia. Tel. (988) 71 18 97.
- *Federación Tinerfeña de Montañismo,* San Sebastián 76, Santa Cruz de Tenerife. Tel. (922) 24 20 44.
- *Federación Valenciana de Montañismo,* Castellón 12, 4.°, 16.ª, Valencia 4. Tel. (96) 321 93 58.
- *Federación Vaso-Navarra de Montañismo,* Avenida Navarra 25, Hotel Urteaga, Beasaín (Guipúzcoa). Tel. (943) 88 08 50.
- *Ferrocariles de Montaña de Grandes Pendientes,* P° de Gracia 26, Barcelona 7. Tel. (93) 301 97 77. For information on snow conditions: Tel. (972) 72 72 50.
- *Formigal, S.A.,* Costa 3, Zaragoza. Tel. (974) 48 81 25. For information on snow conditions: Tel. (974) 48 81 25 or 48 81 26.

G

- *GEO CENTER,* Internationales Landkartenhaus, Honigwiesenstrasse 25, Postfach 80 08 30, D-7000 Stuttgart, Germany. Tel. (0711) 73 50 31.

I

- *Instituto Geográfico Nacional,* Calle General Ibanez de Ibero 3, Madrid 3. Tel. (91) 233 38 00.

L

- *La Flecha de Oro,* two locations: Estudios 9-1.ª Planta, Madrid 12, Tel. (91) 265 33 30 and Plaza de Cascorro 3, Madrid 5, Tel. (91) 227 28 59.
- *La Pinilla,* Avenida Generalíssimo 81, Madrid 16. Tel. (91) 279 57 83.
- *Librería Deportiva,* Plaza Pontejos 2. Madrid 12. Tel. (91) 221 38 68.
- *Librería Esteban Sanz,* Plaza Plaza Pontejos 2, Madrid 12.
- *Librería Gema,* Milicias Nacionales 3, Oviedo.
- *Lles de Cerdanya,* Lles (Lérida). Tel. (973) 64 00 25.
- *Llibreria Quera,* Petritxol 2, Barcelona 2. Tel. (93) 318 07 43.

M

- *Masella,* P° de Gracia 30, Barcelona 7. Tel. (93) 318 26 46. For information on snow conditions, highway conditions and weather: Tel. (972) 89 01 06.
- *Montañas de Trevinca, S.A.,* two locations: General Aranda 72, Vigo (Pontevedra) and Barco de Valdeorras (Orense).

O

- **Oficina de Información de Turismo:**
  — *Albacete:* Avenida Rodríquez Acosta 3, Albacete. Tel. (967) 22 33 80.
  — *Alicante:* Esplanada de España 2, Alicante. Tel. (965) 21 22 85.
  — *Almería:* Avenida Generalíssimo Franco 115, Almería. Tel. (951) 23 47 05.
  — *Avila:* Plaza de la Catedral 4, Avila. Tel. (918) 21 13 87.
  — *Barcelona:* Avenida José Antonio 658, Barcelona. Tel. (93) 222 11 35, 222 12 08 or 317 22 46.
  — *Bilbao:* Alameda Mazarredo 3 n., Bilbao. Tel. 423 64 30.
  — *Burgos:* Paseo del Espolón 1, Burgos. Tel. (947) 20 18 46.
  — *Castellón de la Plana:* Plaza Maria Augustina 5 bajo, Castellón de la Plana. Tel. (964) 22 77 03.
  — *Cuenca:* Colon 34, Cuenca· Tel. (966) 22 23 31.
  — *Girona:* Ciudadanos 12, Girona Tel. (972) 20 16 94.
  — *Granada:* Casa de los Teiros, Granada. Tel. (958) 22 10 22.
  — *Guadalajara:* Trav. Beladiez 1, Guadalajara. Tel. (911) 22 09 59 or 22 06 98.

— *Huesca:* Coso Alto 35, Huesca. Tel. (974) 22 57 78.

— *Jaen:* Arguitecito Bergés 3, Jaen. Tel. (953) 22 27 37.

— *La Coruña:* Dársena de la Marina, La Coruña. Tel. (981) 22 18 22.

— *León:* Plaza de Regla 4, León. Tel. (987) 23 70 82.

— *Lérida:* Instituto de Estudios Llerdenses, Plaza de la Catedral, s/n., Lérida, Tel. (973) 21 17 82 and Avenida Blondel 62, Lérida, Tel. (973) 22 07 79.

— *Logroño:* Miguel Villanueva 10, Logroño. Tel. (941) 21 54 97.

— *Lugo:* Plaza de España 27, Lugo. Tel. (982) 21 13 61.

— *Madrid:* Alcalá 44, Madrid. Tel. (91) 221 12 68. Branch offices are also located at: Aeropuerto Barajas, Tel. (91) 205 12 22; Estacion Chamartin, Tel. (91) 733 10 20; and Princesa 1 (Torre), Tel. (91) 241 12 325.

— *Malaga:* Larios 5, Malaga. Tel. (952) 21 35 45.

— *Murcia:* Glorieta de España 1, Murcia. Tel. (968) 21 37 16.

— *Orense:* Curros Enriquez 1, Orense. Tel. (988) 21 50 75.

— *Oviedo:* Cabo Naval 5, Oviedo. Tel. (985) 21 33 85.

— *Palencia:* Mayor 153, Palencia. Tel. (998) 72 07 77.

— *Pamplona:* Duque de Ahumada 3, Pamplona. Tel. (948) 21 12 87.

— *Pirineos (Lérida):* Alto Aran, Pirineos (Lérida). Tel. (973) 65 00 25.

— *Pontevedra:* General Mola 1, Pontevedra. Tel. (986) 85 08 14.

— *Santander:* Plaza Vezarde 1, Santander. Tel. 21 14 17.

— *San Sebastián:* Andía 13, San Sebastián. Tel. (943) 41 17 74.

— *Segovia:* Plaza General Franco 8, Segovia. Tel. (911) 41 16 02.

— *Soria:* Plaza Ramón Y Cajal, Soria. Tel. (975) 21 20 52.

— *Tarragona:* Rambla del Generalíssimo 50, Tarragona. Tel. (977) 20 18 59.

— *Teruel:* Tomás Nougués 1, Teruel. Tel. (974) 60 22 79.

— *Valencia:* Calle de la Paz 46, Valencia. Tel. (96) 321 25 85.

— *Vitoria:* Dato 17, Vitoria. Tel. 23 25 79.

— *Zaragoza:* Torreón de la Zuda, Zaragoza. Tel. (976) 23 00 27.

P

• *Pallars Turistico,* Calle Provenza 264, Barcelona 8. Tel. (93) 215 55 35. For information on snow conditions: Tel. (93) 215 55 35. For reservations and information: Tel. (973) 62 01 96.

- *Panticosa Turistica,* Calle Cádiz 7, Zaragoza. Tel. (976) 22 92 62. For information on snow conditions: (974) 48 81 25 or 48 81 26.
- *Pistas Sant Joan de L'Erm,* Seo de Urgel (Lérida).
- *Port del Comte,* Apartado de Correos, 26, Solsona (Lérida). Recorded message: Tel. (93) 811 04 81.
- *Promociones Turisticas del Pirineo, S.A.,* Vía Layotana 26, Barcelona. Tel. Bohí (Lérida) 25.
- *Puigmal,* Floridablance 122, Barcelona 11. Tel. (93) 224 08 20.

R

- *Red Española de Albergues Juveniles* (Spanish Youth Hostel Association), José Ortega y Gasset 71, Madrid 6. Tel. (91) 401 13 00.
- *Refugio Caro:* see *Unió Excursionista de Catalunya, Tortosa.*
- *Refugio del AAEEMI,* Miramar. Tel. (977) 60 01 06. Sr. Güell de Valls.
- *Refugio Mustí-Recasens,* Mont-ral. Tel. (977) 30 19 39.

S

- *Sanjust,* Canuda 6, Barcelona 2. Tel. (93) 302 36 95.
- *Secretaria de Estado del Turismo,* Alcalá 44, Madrid 14. Tel. (91) 222 83 70 or 221 12 68.
- *Spanish National Tourist Office,* 57-58 St. James Street, London SW1A 1LD England. Tel. (01) 499 1095 or 499 0901.
- *Spanish National Tourist Office,* 665 Fifth Avenue, New York, New York, 10022 U.S.A. Tel. (212) 759-8822.
- *Sports Alp,* Avinguda de Gaudi 36, Barcelona. Tel. (93) 236 46 43.
- *Super-Espot,* Avenida Generalíssimo 614-616, Barcelona 15. Tel. (93) 322 00 53.

T

- *Telesquis Pirenaicos,* Calle Julían Portet 3, Barcelona 2. Tel. (93) 302 18 20 or 89 20 11.
- *Transportes Aereos del Guadarrama,* Calle Casado del Alisal 7, Madrid 14. Tel. (91) 239 07 74 and 230 55 72. Permanent information numbers: Tel. (91) 852 08 57 and 852 14 35.
- *Tuca,* Calle San Nicolas 4.-1°-B, Viella (Lérida), Tel. Viella (Lérida) 221 or Calle Maestro Falla 1, Barcelona 17. Tel. (93) 203 61 17. For information on snow conditions: Tel. Viella (Lérida) 221.

U

- *Unió Excursionista de Catalunya,* Avenida José Antonio 580, Barcelona 11. Tel. (93) 254 32 47.
- *Unió Excursionista de Catalunya,* Torlosa: Calle Arc Romeu 6, Tortosa.

V

- *Valdezcaray, S.A.,* Calle Travesía del Tenorio 8, Ezcaray (Logroño). Tel. (041) 275. For information on snow conditions: Tel. Ezcaray (041) 275.
- *Vall Ter, S.A.,* Calle Valencia 1, Comprodon (Gerona). Tel. (972) 23 80 04. For information: Tel. (972) 74 00 41 or 74 01 22.

W

- *Weather Forecasts:* Tel. (91) 244 35 00 or, for recorded forecasts, Tel. (91) 232 35 00.
- *West Col Productions,* 1 Meadow Close, Goring-on-Thames, Reading, Berkshire RG8 9AA, England.

A Quick Reference

In a hurry? Turn to the pages listed below. They will give you the most important information on walking in Spain.

About the Author

CRAIG EVANS is an avid walker, winter mountaineer, writer, editor and photographer. He worked his way through college as a reporter for the *San Jose Mercury-News* in San Jose, California, and wrote an award-winning student travel publication, *Tripping*, which was distributed through West Coast student travel offices from 1973 to 1975. Mr. Evans then spent a year as editor of BACKPACKER Magazine and was project editor for the revised edition of BACKPACKER's *Backpacking Equipment Buyer's Guide* (a comprehensive, 285-page book that includes articles on how virtually every type of hiking equipment is made, as well as individual product reports on more than 1,000 pieces of gear). He has written articles on walking and traveling in Europe, and compiled reports on lightweight stoves, binoculars, winter tents and winter footwear for the equipment sections in BACKPACKER Magazine.

Mr. Evans visited Europe for the first time in 1971, and during the next two years traveled and walked in virtually every one of the Western European countries. He has since returned to Europe six times.

In 1973, he spent six months in the Alps, walking more than 2,000 kilometers (1,300 miles) from Menton, France, to Trieste, Italy. He has also led walking tours in the Alps.

For the *On Foot Through Europe* series, Mr. Evans worked for three years compiling information, checking facts and writing. He visited virtually every one of Europe's major walking organizations and alpine clubs, taking time to accompany members on the trails they know best. In the end, he had collected more than 450 kilos (half a ton) of information in 12 languages—the information from which this book was distilled.

To this, he added the experience gained backpacking in the East and West coast mountains of the United States, the Arizona desert and the Canadian Rockies.

Born in Klamath Falls, Oregon, in 1949, he holds a Bachelor of Arts degree in English from the California State University, San Jose. He now lives in Washington, D.C.